Cultivating and Keeping
Committed Special Education Teachers

This book is dedicated to my husband, Randy, and to my children, Evan and Lauren.

Cultivating and Keeping
Committed Special Education Teachers

What Principals and District Leaders Can Do

Bonnie S. Billingsley
Foreword by James McLeskey

A Joint Publication

CORWIN PRESS
A SAGE Publications Company
Thousand Oaks, California

Council for
Exceptional
Children

For information:

Corwin Press
A Sage Publications Company
2455 Teller Road
Thousand Oaks, California 91320
www.corwinpress.com

Sage Publications Ltd.
1 Oliver's Yard
55 City Road
London EC1Y 1SP
United Kingdom

Sage Publications India Pvt. Ltd.
B-42, Panchsheel Enclave
Post Box 4109
New Delhi 110 017 India

Printed in the United States of America.

Library of Congress Cataloging-in-Publication Data

Billingsley, Bonnie S.
Cultivating and keeping committed special education teachers : what principals and district leaders can do / Bonnie S. Billingsley.
    p. cm.
"A joint publication with the Council for Exceptional Children."
Includes bibliographical references and index.
ISBN 1-4129-0887-6 (cloth) — ISBN 1-4129-0888-4 (pbk.)
    1. Teachers of children with disabilities—In-service training.
2. Teachers of children with disabilities—Vocational guidance. I. Title.
LC4019.8.B55 2005
371.9—dc22

                                                    2004025069

This book is printed on acid-free paper.

05   06   07   08   09   10   9   8   7   6   5   4   3   2   1

Acquisitions Editor:	Robert D. Clouse
Editorial Assistant:	Jingle Vea
Production Editor:	Sanford Robinson
Copy Editor:	David Yurkovich
Typesetter:	C&M Digitals (P) Ltd.
Proofreader:	Eileen Delaney
Indexer:	Naomi Linzer
Cover Designer:	Anthony Paular

Contents

List of Figures

List of Contributors

Dr. Lynn Boyer, West Virginia Department of Education

Dr. Mary T. Brownell, University of Florida

Dr. Lynne Cook, California State University, Northridge

Dr. Jean B. Crockett, Virginia Tech

Dr. Elizabeth Hess Rice, George Washington University

Ms. Cyndi Pitonyak, Montgomery County Public Schools, Blacksburg, Virginia

Dr. Michael S. Rosenberg, Johns Hopkins University

Dr. Paul T. Sindelar, University of Florida

Foreword

Currently the U.S. educational system is marked by significant controversy, as increasingly higher student achievement outcomes are sought for all students, including those with disabilities. While there is much controversy regarding the particular approaches that should be used to improve outcomes, all seem to agree that teachers are the single most important influence on student achievement. Sanders and colleagues (Sanders & Rivers, 1996; Wright, Horn, & Sanders, 1997) have made this point most boldly, in noting that, over a period of years the quality of the general education teacher contributes more to student achievement than *any other factor*, including class size, class composition, or student background. More specifically, their research has demonstrated that students who are assigned to the most effective general education teachers for three consecutive years score as many as 50 percentile points higher on achievement measures when compared to students who are assigned to the least effective teachers during a comparable period.

There seems little doubt that special education teachers are at least as important as general educators—perhaps more so—in ensuring high achievement levels for students with disabilities. Students with disabilities are only labeled once they have failed to make adequate progress in a general education teacher's classroom. Thus, in addition to the skills and knowledge that are required of a highly qualified general education classroom teacher, special education teachers are required to have specialized skills for addressing unique student needs; extensive knowledge of highly effective, evidence-based practices; and the ability to collaborate effectively with other teachers to ensure that students with disabilities make academic and social progress that enables them to be successful in life. In short, special education teachers are the key to ensuring a high-quality education and good achievement outcomes for students with disabilities.

Despite the widely recognized need for highly qualified special education teachers, we have been unsuccessful in ensuring an adequate supply of these teachers for America's classrooms. In the fifty states and the

District of Columbia, approximately 400,000 special education teachers are hired each year to teach school-age students with disabilities. During the 2001–2002 school year (the most recent available data from the U.S. Department of Education [www.ideadata.org]), over 12% of these teachers, serving over 900,000 students with disabilities lacked the basic certification to effectively meet student needs. The shortage of fully certified teachers in special education has grown significantly in recent years, and is now greater than any other area of certification, including the more widely publicized shortages of math and science teachers (McLeskey, Tyler, & Flippin, 2004).

Adding to the problem of ensuring that all students with disabilities have highly qualified teachers is a high attrition rate among special education teachers (Boe, Bobbitt, Cook, & Barkanic, 1998; Boe, Bobbitt, Cook, Barkanic, & Maislin, 1999). Within four years of beginning to teach, over one-half of all special education teachers either leave the profession altogether or transfer to general education. Perhaps as important, during this same four-year period, those who remain in special education frequently migrate from one school to another, seeking a more satisfying role and better working conditions. More specifically, every four years, approximately 40% of all special education teachers move from one school to another, either within their current district or without. Finally, perhaps the most alarming statistic regarding special education teacher attrition, is the transfer rate to general education. Special educators are ten times more likely to transfer to general education as general educators are to transfer to special education (McLeskey, Tyler, & Flippin, 2004). If this statistic were reversed (i.e., ten times more general educators transferring into special education), the special education teacher shortage would not exist.

These statistics reveal an extraordinarily high level of instability in the special education teaching profession, resulting in teachers moving in and out of special education classrooms at a disquieting rate. Teacher attrition, coupled with migration from school to school, has a significant adverse effect on student outcomes. For example, we know that it takes four to six years to become an accomplished teacher—many special education teachers do not remain in the profession long enough to reach this level of competence. We also know that effective special education teachers collaborate with other educators to change their schools to ensure that the needs of students with disabilities are met. It often takes five or more years for these changes to occur, and most special education teachers do not remain in one school for this period of time. Thus, special education teachers often do not remain in a school or the profession for a long enough period to either become an accomplished professional or to work toward the necessary changes in a school to ensure the success of students with disabilities.

Although these statistics can be quite depressing, it is important to remember that at least in one important sense they are "just statistics." While they reveal important trends, they do not reveal the reality that exists in every school in America. Moreover, there are many schools with dedicated, highly qualified special education teachers who remain in their positions for many years and achieve extraordinary outcomes for students with disabilities. For example, my colleagues and I have worked with many schools on school improvement-related activities, and these schools invariably have had a highly qualified special education faculty that have remained at their schools over a long period of time. Clearly, the single most important factor in these schools that ensures a strong, stable special education faculty is a supportive school principal (McLeskey & Waldron, 2000, 2002). What these principals seem to do is to provide a context in which special education teachers have a manageable role that allows them to achieve the moral purpose for which they entered teaching (i.e., to make a difference in the lives of the students they teach).

Over the last fifteen years, our knowledge has advanced to the point where we have a relatively strong knowledge base regarding how to recruit highly qualified special education teachers into the classroom and keep them there. For example, we recognize that beginning teachers are, in fact, novice teachers; they are not accomplished professionals. Thus, novice educators need strong induction programs, a mentor or mentors to work with as they learn about their school and teaching, and ongoing professional development tailored to their unique context and needs. Unfortunately, this knowledge base is often not translated into practice.

Bonnie Billingsley has done an exceptional job of synthesizing and applying available research in this book, while offering a range of effective and proven strategies that principals and district administrators can use as they seek to identify, recruit, support, and retain highly qualified special education teachers in their schools. I am hopeful that many principals and district administrators who seek to improve outcomes for students with disabilities will read this book and incorporate many of the ideas presented. Indeed, these strategies offer principals the potential to provide a grassroots support system for ensuring that all students with disabilities have highly qualified teachers and achieve outcomes that result in success in school, thus creating many options for a successful life beyond school.

James McLeskey
Professor and Chair, Department of
Special Education, University of Florida

REFERENCES

Boe, E., Bobbitt, S., Cook, L., & Barkanic, G. (1998). *National Trends in Teacher Supply and Turnover* (Data analysis report no. 1998 DAR1). Philadelphia, PA: University of Pennsylvania, Graduate School of Education, Center for Research and Evaluation in Social Policy.

Boe, E., Bobbitt, S., Cook, L., Barkanic, G., & Maislin, G. (1999). *Teacher Turnover in Eight Cognate Areas: National Trends and Predictors.* (Data analysis report no. 1998 DAR3). Philadelphia, PA: University of Pennsylvania, Graduate School of Education, Center for Research and Evaluation in Social Policy.

McLeskey, J., Tyler, N., & Flippin, S. (2004). The supply of and demand for special education teachers: A review of research regarding the nature of the chronic shortage of special education teachers. *Journal of Special Education, 38*(1), 5–21.

McLeskey, J., & Waldron, N. (2002). School change and inclusive schools: Lessons learned from practice. *Phi Delta Kappan, 84*(1), 65–72.

McLeskey, J., & Waldron, N. (2000). *Inclusive Education in Action: Making Differences Ordinary.* Alexandria, VA: ASCD.

Sanders, W., & Rivers, J. (1996). *Cumulative and Residual Effects of Teachers on Future Student Academic Achievement.* Knoxville, TN: University of Tennessee Value-Added Research and Assessment Center.

Wright, S., Horn, S., & Sanders, W. (1997). Teacher and classroom context effects on student achievement: Implication for teacher evaluation. *Journal of Personnel Evaluation in Education, 11*, 57–67.

Preface

Why do so many special educators leave their positions each year? How can we reduce attrition? I have asked these questions over the last twenty-five years in my work as a special education administrator and as a university faculty member. Some teacher attrition is natural and positive. New teachers can bring innovative ideas and help others look at things in new ways. It is also best for those not suited for teaching careers to leave. However, each year many special education teachers who entered the field with a great deal of enthusiasm leave because of poor working conditions and inadequate supports. Some stay in their schools, but transfer to general education positions. A higher percentage of special educators leave than any group of general educators, including math and science teachers. Replacing these teachers is disruptive for schools and a challenging problem in an era of teacher shortage.

Specific problems in special educators' work lives contribute to attrition. Some of these problems are obvious, such as the extensive bureaucratic and legal requirements of special education teaching. Others are more subtle and reflect the differences between special and general education teacher cultures and feelings of isolation. Lack of administrative support is an attrition factor that is emphasized in many special education studies.

As a former special education supervisor, I worked with many principals across elementary and secondary schools. Principals, perhaps more than any other school personnel, influence whether special educators want to stay in their schools. The work that principals do as leaders influences the climate for special education in the school, whether teachers have opportunities to collaborate, and how well they are able to address students' needs.

Most principals are caring and motivated individuals who want to support teachers and foster student learning. Yet, many principals find dealing with special education a daunting task, fraught with legal mine fields. School leaders have numerous questions about the discipline of students with disabilities, how to make sure compliance issues are addressed, and how to avoid the next due process hearing. So, it's no surprise that the support of special education teachers isn't always a top concern.

Many school leaders have had no systematic preparation to prepare them to create effective educational environments for students with disabilities. Often school leaders are left to learn many aspects of special education on their own. When principals do provide assistance, it is often focused on the legal aspects of special education, rather than how to foster special educators' professional growth or address the needs of students with disabilities. High demands on principals' time, coupled with the problems inherent in administering special education programs, makes for a frustrating experience.

Leaders have asked me numerous questions about special education teacher attrition over the years. For example: "Why are special education teachers leaving in droves?" "What do special educators mean by the lack of administrative support?" and "What can we do to have some stability in special education?"

Principals can do a great deal to retain special educators. These teachers indicate that a supportive principal is the *number one* incentive for staying in special education. Numerous studies show that teachers who perceive their principals as supportive experience higher job satisfaction, greater commitment, more colleague support, fewer work problems, and less stress and burnout than those who are not supported.

This book provides a framework and specific guidelines for increasing special education teacher retention. The central premise of this book is that when principals work to create school environments in which special educators feel supported and can use their expertise to help students with disabilities achieve, they are also creating the conditions that facilitate teacher satisfaction, commitment, and retention. Some of the recommendations presented in this book take considerable effort and thought. Others are relatively simple and can be implemented immediately. The guidelines presented in this book are part of what the best leaders do— "great school leaders create nurturing school environments in which accomplished teaching can flourish and grow" (Darling-Hammond, 2003, p. 3).

Cultivating and keeping committed special educators is also an important responsibility of district leaders. Principals cannot do all of the work by themselves. Many of the ideas presented in this book can be considered from a school or district perspective. For example, both principals and school leaders need to share responsibility for recruiting, hiring, inducting, and providing effective professional development.

District administrators are often in a better position than principals to communicate with state departments of education to consider specifically how state leadership can support school and district efforts. Specifically, the state Comprehensive System of Personnel Development (CSPD) under the Individuals with Disabilities Education Act (1997) supports the recruitment, retention, and professional growth of teachers. State leadership can also help with regulating special educators' caseloads, reducing the bureaucratic demands on teachers, and supporting special education teacher induction.

PURPOSES AND GOALS OF THIS BOOK

The primary purpose of this book is to help school and district leaders understand the factors that influence attrition as well as what they can do to retain special education teachers. This book provides specific recommendations for developing highly qualified special educators and providing the conditions in which they can succeed and grow professionally. Although this book is written with the special education teacher in mind, some of the recommendations apply to general educators as well.

More specifically, this book provides:

1. A broad framework that leaders can use to see the "big picture" of teacher retention,

2. A perspective of the specific work problems that lead special educators to resign, and

3. Specific guidelines to improve special educators' retention.

AUDIENCES FOR THIS BOOK

This book is appropriate for several audiences: leaders, mentors, and faculty members. Each of these groups has a stake in improving teacher quality and helping special educators develop satisfying work lives. Thus, the following audiences will find this book helpful:

- **_Principals and Assistant Principals:_** School leaders are in a key position to facilitate special education teacher retention. They are critical to the creation of a positive school climate for all teachers and students, and set the tone for how students with disabilities are served in schools.

- *District Leaders:* District personnel, such as directors, supervisors, and coordinators of special education, are in an important position to assess teacher needs across the district. Without careful coordination and planning between school and district leaders, critical leadership tasks may be overlooked.

- *Mentors and Teacher Leaders:* Mentors and teacher leaders will develop a better understanding of the needs of beginning teachers, how roles can be clarified, and how to help new teachers reduce their stress levels. They will also develop an understanding of effective leadership in special education and acquire an understanding of how to facilitate the professional development of others.

- *Human Resources Administrators:* The material on recruiting and hiring, teacher induction, stress management, and systematic planning efforts to understand and reduce district attrition should be relevant to these leaders.

- *Faculty in Colleges and Universities:* College and university professors searching for a text on the school and district leaders' roles in improving special education practices can use this book as supplementary text in educational leadership.

- *Leaders in State Departments of Education and Union Leaders:* There is a role to be played by state departments of education and unions in supporting teachers and promoting wellness. For example, induction programs, work assignments, and teacher wellness can be promoted by these groups. The CSPD that is part of the Individuals with Disabilities Education Act (IDEA) can provide districts with resources to implement some of the strategies identified in this book.

ORGANIZATION OF THIS BOOK

Part I of the book addresses understanding special education teacher attrition and retention. Chapter 1 introduces the topic and provides a Leader's Framework for Cultivating and Keeping Special Education Teachers. Figure 1.1 provides a visual organizer for the chapters that follow. The second chapter briefly reviews the growing literature on special education attrition and summarizes the research findings in a table. In particular, Chapter 2 provides a picture of what contributes to special educators' feelings of being unsupported and overwhelmed in their schools.

Part II of the book addresses finding and cultivating high-quality special educators. Chapters 3–5 consider how to increase the quantity and quality of special education teachers in schools in ways that will increase their likelihood of staying. The basic premise underlying these chapters is that well-qualified teachers who have the expertise needed for their work and who are well matched to their positions will be more likely to stay.

Part III addresses how to create positive work environments. Chapters 6–8 provide specific recommendations for improving teachers' work conditions and decreasing teacher stress. Finally, Chapter 9 outlines a process that leaders can use to assess what is contributing to attrition in their districts and a strategic planning process to improve these conditions.

Part IV provides numerous resources and specific assessments that leaders can use to better understand the local conditions that influence teacher attrition.

Following Chapter 1, each chapter uses the following format:

- Brief introduction and scenario,
- Chapter overview,
- A brief link between chapter topic and what we know about teacher attrition and retention,
- Primary content of the chapter,
- Tips for leaders,
- A bulleted summary of major chapter themes, and
- Selected readings and Web sites.

A feedback form is provided at the end of the book. I am interested in your ideas, comments, and suggestions (bbilling@vt.edu).

Acknowledgments

I gratefully acknowledge the contributions of the following individuals, each of whom made thoughtful contributions to this book: Lynn Boyer, Mary Brownell, Lynne Cook, Jean Crockett, Elizabeth Hess Rice, Cyndi Pitonyak, Michael Rosenberg, and Paul Sindelar. My thanks are also extended to James McLeskey, for encouraging me to write this book and for providing its Foreword. I extend a special thanks to my colleague and friend, Dr. Jean Crockett, for her careful reading and thoughtful comments on the initial manuscript. Jean also helped me with the title of this book as she provided the words "Cultivate and Keep" (Crockett, 2004, p. 189).

I am especially grateful and indebted to my family for their loving support through this entire process. Specifically, my husband, Randy, edited my initial manuscript; my daughter, Lauren, was a careful reader and a great reference checker; and my son, Evan, was especially patient as I took too many evenings to finish this book.

Corwin Press gratefully acknowledges the contribution of the following people:

Kathie Dobberteen
Principal
Highlands Elementary School
Bonita, CA

Ronald K. Felton
Associate Superintendent
Miami-Dade County Schools
Miami, FL

Michelle Gayle
Principal
Griffin Middle School
Tallahassee, FL

Mark J. Rendell
Principal
Titusville High School
Titusville, FL

Scott Hollinger
Principal
McAuliffe Elementary School
McAllen, TX

Steven M. Laub
Principal
Rolla Junior High School
Rolla, MO

Debi B. Phillips
Associate Principal
South Oldham Middle School
Crestwood, KY

Wendy Dallman
Special Education Teacher
New London High School
New London, WI

Don Poplau
Principal
Mankato East High School
Mankato, MN

Larry Birdsell
Principal
Conejo Elementary School
Thousand Oaks, CA

James McLeskey
Professor and Chair
Department of Special
    Education
University of Florida
Gainesville, FL

John W. Somers
Associate Professor of Teacher
    Education
University of Indianapolis
Indianapolis, IN

Harriet Gould
Principal
Raymond Central Elementary
    Schools
Valparaiso, NE

Melba Fletcher
Director of Graduate
    Internships
Graduate Teacher
    Education Program
Fischler Graduate School of
    Education
Nova Southeastern
    University
North Miami Beach, FL

Teri Wallace
Research Associate
College of Education and
    Human Development
University of Minnesota
Minneapolis, MN

About the Author

Bonnie S. Billingsley is faculty member in he School of Education at Virginia Tech. She has taught a range of courses over the last fifteen years in the areas of learning disabilities, emotional disorders, and the administration and supervision of special education. Dr. Billingsley began her career teaching students with disabilities in Tallahassee and St. Augustine, Florida. She also served as district supervisor of special education in both St. Augustine, Florida, and in Roanoke City, Virginia.

Dr. Billingsley's research interests are in the preparation, support, and retention of special education teachers. Her interests in retention are focused on workplace conditions and the induction of new teachers. Dr. Billingsley has published numerous articles in leading journals on special education teacher retention, teacher support, and the needs of beginning special education teachers. She has served as a consultant in the area of special education teacher retention to various professional organizations, school systems, state departments of education, research groups, and universities; she has been an invited speaker at numerous conferences.

Part I

Understanding Teacher Attrition and Retention

Introduction

1

*A Leader's Framework
for Teacher Retention*

*Keeping good teachers should be one of the most important agenda
items for any school leader.*

(Darling-Hammond, 2003, p. 6)

Principals have a critical role in cultivating and keeping committed special educators. For special educators to do their work well, they need the knowledge, skills, and dispositions for teaching students with disabilities. However, highly qualified teachers are not sufficient for strong programs for students with disabilities. Special educators also need the structures, resources, and supports necessary to carry out their responsibilities. Unfortunately, special educators often are not given the necessary supports, and many leave their positions frustrated and discouraged.

The need for committed special educators suggests the need for a broader definition of retention, one that involves not just retaining all teachers, but also the importance of creating environments that sustain teachers' *commitment* to their work (Gold, 1996). It is essential to create supportive environments where teachers have positive relationships with others and have the work conditions necessary to use effective practices.

CHAPTER OVERVIEW

In this era of teacher shortage, school and district leaders need to ask what they can do to retain their special educators. This chapter provides a leadership framework for retaining committed special educators and provides an introduction and overview of this book.

THE LEADERSHIP FRAMEWORK

Figure 1.1 shows a "big picture" of factors that influence teacher retention. This framework shows that leaders need to focus on two broad considerations: 1) improving teacher quality, and 2) creating positive work conditions. Qualified special educators who work in productive and supportive schools are better able to help students succeed, to know that their teaching efforts have made a difference, and to experience job satisfaction. Teachers who experience these rewards are more likely to be committed to and remain in their jobs (Billingsley, 2004). In contrast, poor work conditions lead teachers to feel that their efforts do not make a difference (e.g., low self-efficacy). It is these feelings of "inconsequentiality" that lead to stress and burnout (Farber, 2000).

Figure 1.1 highlights specific aspects of the work environment that can be altered to improve teacher retention. These *retention-enhancing* actions also describe the conditions for effective programs for students with disabilities. Although aspects of the model add work and expense, some are less than the costs of high turnover. For example, the costs of induction are substantially less than the costs associated with high turnover (Benner, 2000).

The actions in Figure 1.1 are an integral part of what strong leaders do. Even in times of teacher surplus—these factors remain a necessary part of good leadership. Leaders need to assess local circumstances that are contributing to teacher attrition and strategically determine priorities for change. The questions, assessment instruments, and strategic planning model presented in Chapter 9 can be used to assess needs for change.

Approaches to teacher retention that are piecemeal and address only one aspect of the model will yield disappointing results. For example, induction programs will not have a major effect on retention if work conditions are very poor.

Improving Teacher Quality

Figure 1.1 emphasizes the importance of improving teacher quality through: 1) careful recruitment and hiring practices, 2) responsive induction programs for new teachers, and 3) effective professional development opportunities. Chapters 3–5 provide recommendations to address each of these three key areas.

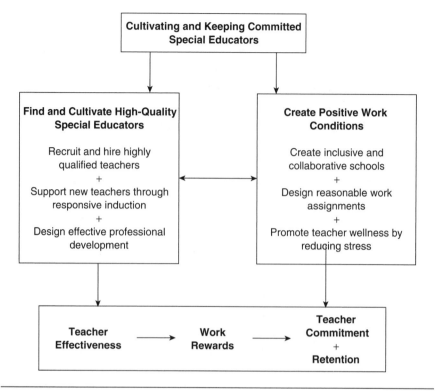

Figure 1.1   A Leader's Framework for Teacher Retention

Recruit and Hire High-Quality Special Educators

The recruitment, hiring, and placement of new teachers can affect teacher retention. Attention to early and systematic recruitment and hiring processes can help leaders find the best possible match for new hires. Thoughtful hiring practices can also assist candidates in making decisions about whether the offered position is a good one for them.

High-Quality Teachers: How Will Leaders Identify Them?

Mary T. Brownell*

The quality of our nation's teachers is essential to ensuring that students reach their academic potential. Without effective teachers, it is likely that many of our nation's youngsters will be left behind academically, particularly those attending high-poverty and minority schools. Over the past decade, researchers have demonstrated that effective teachers can secure better achievement gains than their less effective colleagues. Over a three-year period, researchers demonstrated that the most effective teachers could secure percentile gains on standardized tests that were considerably higher than their least effective colleagues. Clearly, effective teachers differ from their less effective colleagues, but how?

Background characteristics: Effective teachers have certain characteristics that distinguish them from less effective teachers. They are more experienced, academically able, and have better preparation. On a whole, a more experienced teacher can secure stronger student achievement gains. Each year secondary teachers teach, their student achievement scores increase accordingly. The relationship, however, between achievement and elementary teachers' experience is slightly different. Elementary teachers show gains similar to secondary teachers in the first five years of their career, and then again after fourteen years. Academic ability also seems to influence a teacher's effectiveness. Teachers who score higher on the verbal portion of the Scholastic Achievement Test (SAT) or Graduate Record Exam (GRE) are more likely to secure better student achievement gains in reading. Likewise, teachers who score higher on the quantitative portion are more likely to secure better student achievement gains in mathematics. Additionally, graduates of more prestigious colleges and universities are also able to secure better student achievement scores. These findings are more pronounced in high-poverty schools where academically able teachers are able to secure even better student achievement gains than they can with the larger school population. Teachers who are prepared to do their jobs also seem to secure better achievement gains. Although findings from the certification literature are mixed, the majority of research studies suggest that certified teachers are more capable of securing better student achievement gains than their uncertified counterparts. Moreover, recent findings from a study of exemplary teacher education programs shows that beginning teachers who received outstanding initial preparation in reading pedagogy were able to secure better student gains on tests of reading comprehension than their counterparts who were less well prepared. Finally, intensity of preparation is related to teaching experience. Teachers who graduate from four- and five-year preparation programs along with those who participate in intensive alternative certification routes are far more likely to remain in the classroom than those teachers who enter with three months of preparation or less.

Teacher knowledge: Teachers who are knowledgeable about their content area, pedagogical practices, and students tend to achieve the strongest student achievement gains. Teachers who are prepared in their subject area tend to secure better student achievement than those teachers who lack that preparation, and these findings are the strongest for teachers providing math instruction at the secondary level. However, research also demonstrates that subject matter knowledge is not the only important characteristic of an effective teacher. Teachers who have a major or minor in mathematics and have completed education coursework focused on how to teach mathematics secure better student achievement gains than those teachers who only have subject matter expertise. Additionally, teachers' knowledge of phonological awareness and decoding does not necessarily translate into effective classroom reading practice.

This research demonstrates that teachers know more than just the content they are teaching. They know how to put their content knowledge into practice. Research on teacher thinking shows that expert teachers have a deep understanding of content, pedagogical practices for representing that content, curricular materials, and students. They understand the difficulties students might encounter in learning a subject and how curricular materials and instructional strategies might be useful in responding to those difficulties. These teachers not only know a lot, they also understand what to do with their knowledge in a classroom. This complex interweave of different types of knowledge is something that more novice teachers do not have, particularly those who lack preparation in education. Novice teachers with only subject matter expertise struggle with classroom management and lack the pedagogy for representing their subject matter knowledge to students.

Classroom practices: What classroom teachers do is more related to gains in student achievement than any other facet of teacher quality. A recent study of Nationally Board Certified teachers demonstrated that these teachers were far more effective in securing student achievement gains than teachers who did have certification, and they were particularly effective in raising the achievement levels of students in poverty. These findings suggest that teachers identified as exemplary engage in practices that are more effective than their counterparts who are educated and experienced,

So what is it that effective teachers do? Effective teachers provide active, well-structured instruction that engages students. Additionally, they gear instruction to students' academic abilities. For instance, effective teachers have students reading texts at their reading level rather than insisting that all children read grade level material. Their instruction is rich and dense. A moment is never wasted in effective teachers' classrooms. They teach students concepts and skills that are critical to high performance in a content area and motivate students to participate in their instruction. These teachers also provide instruction that is well integrated and focused. For instance, excellent elementary reading teachers give students many opportunities to read connected text and discuss that text while providing the explicit skill instruction that some students need.

Dispositions: Effective teachers are committed to teaching and believe that they can make a difference in the lives of students. Teachers who are able to secure the strongest student achievement gains, particularly among students who are culturally diverse and those who live in poverty, are the ones who believe that it is their responsibility to help students learn. These teachers do not blame students and their parents for poor achievement but ask themselves what they can do to help their students learn more. It is important, however, to recognize that efficacious teachers have the most influence when they work in a school where there is a collective sense of efficacy and commitment to the students, suggesting that specific qualities of the schoolhouse may matter more in influencing teachers' dispositions rather than what the individual teacher brings to the table.

*Dr. Mary T. Brownell is an associate professor in special education at the University of Florida. She is also codirector of the Center for Personnel Studies in Special Education (COPSSE) see www.copsse.org.

Support New Teachers Through Responsive Induction

Once teachers are hired, carefully designed induction programs are of vital importance to supporting special educators during these early years. Goals for induction programs need to extend beyond helping teachers survive the first teaching years. Induction programs need to facilitate teacher learning and growth, and lead to student achievement. Although many states and districts have programs for new teachers, they may not meet the needs of special educators. Special educators have unique needs and concerns that require specific types of assistance. Chapter 4 reviews the needs of new special educators and the actions that districts can take to create responsive induction programs.

Design Effective Professional Development

All teachers need meaningful learning experiences and opportunities to obtain more knowledge about effective practices. Special education teachers who have greater professional development are more likely to feel satisfied with their jobs and report fewer role problems (Gersten, Keating, Yovanoff, & Harniss, 2001). Although special educators often benefit from professional development opportunities oriented for all teachers, special considerations are required for them to meet specific goals.

Past models of after-school workshops and inservice programs are being replaced with new models of professional development. These new models emphasize the importance of learning communities character-ized by inquiry, reflection, and experimentation (Johnson & Kardos, 2002). Learning communities in special education help improve teachers' practice, increase their sense of efficacy, and prevent burnout (Brownell, Yeager, Rennells, & Riley, 1997). Chapter 5 addresses effective professional develop-ment, highlights university-school collaborations for effective professional development, and suggests ways of providing professional development and teacher leadership opportunities for experienced teachers.

Create Positive Work Conditions

Principals support special educators through fostering positive work environments. Special educators who give their schools positive ratings on school climate are more likely to stay in teaching than those who do not (A High-Quality Teacher for Every Classroom, 2002; Miller, Brownell, & Smith, 1999). A positive work environment provides teach-ers with opportunities for teacher success and satisfaction; in contrast, a deficient one contributes to teacher dissatisfaction (Johnson & Birkeland, 2003a).

School and district leaders need to create collaborative and learning-focused school environments in which all students have opportunities to succeed. Leaders need to direct their attention to: (1) creating inclusive and collaborative schools, (2) designing reasonable work assignments, and (3) promoting wellness by reducing stress. Specifically, Chapters 6–8 answer questions including: What creates positive work conditions for special educators? How can school leaders help create environments conducive to special educators' work and student learning? How can an atmosphere of collegiality and ongoing learning be developed? How can special educators' roles be designed so they can use their expertise? How can special educators' stress be reduced?

Create Inclusive and Collaborative Schools

Leadership for inclusive schools supports not just special educators, but all teachers and staff as they work to meet the needs of students with disabilities in inclusive settings. Principals support the work of teachers and staff when they explicitly recognize the importance of serving students with disabilities, help to create a collaborative work environment in which special and general educators work together toward mutually defined goals, and assure that students with disabilities have access to the general education curriculum (see Chapter 6 for eight critical leadership tasks).

The influence of both principal and colleague support can help reduce special educators' isolation and create a sense of belonging in their schools. The creation of positive collegial relationships is an important aspect of supportive work environments. Relationships based on optimism, trust, openness, and respect provide the foundation for collaboration. There is clear evidence that when principals are supportive, teachers experience less stress, greater job satisfaction, and are more likely to stay in their jobs.

Design Reasonable Work Assignments

Well-designed teaching assignments reduce special education attrition and sustain special educators' involvement and commitment. Teachers need to have opportunities to use their expertise, collaborate with their colleagues to meet the needs of students with disabilities, and be protected from unreasonable workloads. Teachers who have reasonable workloads and adequate supports are less likely to experience stress, and are more likely to achieve their goals and experience job satisfaction (Cross & Billingsley, 1994; Gersten et al., 2001). These teachers are also more likely to be effective and experience the intrinsic rewards of teaching.

Promote Wellness by Reducing Stress

Attending to the first five activities in the model will go a long way toward preventing stress and burnout in special education teachers. Another approach is to help teachers develop awareness of their own stress, what contributes to everyday stress, and to develop strategies for coping with the strains of work life.

In summary, the above six conditions help create the circumstances in which special educators will see their students succeed. Why teachers stay is linked to the "knowledge that they are making a difference. . . . Doing work that feels good goes hand in hand with doing good work" (Williams, 2003, p. 74).

TYPES OF ATTRITION: A DISTRICT AND SCHOOL PERSPECTIVE

There are different types of teacher attrition; terms for attrition include leaving, moving, switching, transferring, exiting, and turnover. These attrition labels have different meanings, depending on how they are used. Although teacher attrition can be viewed from the perspective of school, district, state, or the entire national teaching force, this book takes the perspective of school and district attrition, since the loss of teachers from schools and districts is the primary perspective of interest to school and district leaders.

This book is concerned with voluntary attrition. Figure 1.2 provides a description of two major types of district attrition: "Leavers" refer to those who exit the district, while "transfers" refer to those who stay in the district, but take different positions. Both types of attrition influence the need for special educators, and understanding these various types of attrition can help principals and district leaders recognize possible avenues for increasing retention. Teachers who move to neighboring districts may have different reasons for leaving than those who stay in the district but transfer to general education classrooms.

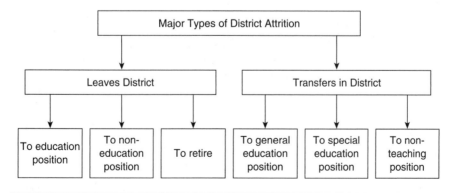

Figure 1.2 Major Types of District Attrition

SOURCE: Recruiting and Retaining High Quality Teachers, the SPeNSF Report. Carlson, 2002.

Leavers

Leavers are a loss to the district because they must be replaced. Unlike teachers who transfer, they do not serve the system in any other capacity. There are three types of leavers:

- Leave district, but not education;
- Leave education; and
- Leave to retire.

Transfers

Teachers who transfer within the district are usually not as much of a concern as other leavers since they remain in the district. Leavers include:

- Transfers from special to general education positions;
- Transfers to another special education position in district; and
- Transfers to a nonteaching position in district.

The first category includes those who transfer from special to general education positions. Special educators are about ten times more likely to transfer to general education positions than the reverse (Boe, Bobbitt, Cook, & Barkanic, 1998). A move to general education has both positive and negative consequences. For example, special educators moving into general education positions may enjoy the change and new responsibilities. Both their students and colleagues will benefit from their expertise. However, in spite of these positives, the special education teacher must still be replaced. Special educators who leave for general education teaching indicate they may be willing to return if they have the possibility of administrative support and better work conditions (Billingsley & Cross, 1991).

The teacher in the second transfer category stays in special education teaching, but moves to another position. Leaders may transfer a teacher because they have a particular need in a different school and/or special education program. For example, the director of special education may ask a teacher to move to a middle school special education position from an elementary program. Leaders need to exercise care in these transfers, because if the move is not truly voluntary, the teacher may leave. Alternatively, a special education teacher may request a transfer to another special education position because he or she is either dissatisfied or has another reason for the transfer (e.g., desires to work with older students, wants to work closer to home). Granting such a transfer in this case may help keep that teacher in the district, even if the particular school loses a teacher.

Teachers in the third category of transfer move to nonteaching positions within the district. Teachers may move to curriculum or leadership positions to meet other needs within the district. Although this represents a teaching loss to both the school and district, these types of moves are beneficial since they meet both individual and district needs. Chapter 9 describes strategies for assessing the impact of different kinds of attrition on the district, as well as specific strategies for gathering information for strategic planning.

CHAPTER SUMMARY

- The leadership framework for improving teacher retention requires attention to both improving teacher quality and creating positive work conditions.
- Retention-enhancing actions serve as important forms of teacher support and help to create strong programs for students with disabilities.
- Improving teacher quality includes directing efforts toward: recruiting and hiring high-quality teachers, establishing strong induction programs, and providing high-quality professional development opportunities.
- Developing positive work environments requires a focus on creating inclusive and collaborative schools, designing reasonable work assignments for special educators, and promoting wellness by reducing stress.

Why Special Educators Leave and Why It Matters

2

Current special education teaching conditions have pushed the field into crisis . . . with special education teachers leaving the profession in record numbers.

("Special Education Teaching
Conditions Must Be Improved," 2000, p. 1)

Nationally, between 7 and 15% of special education teachers leave each year, depending on the definition of attrition used (McLeskey, Tyler, & Flippin, 2004). If 10% leave each year, administrators will have to replace half of their special educators in just a five-year period.

Replacing special education teachers is no easy task and trends suggest it will only be more difficult in the future. The No Child Left Behind [NCLB] Act of 2001 adds to the pressure of finding qualified teachers. More than ever, school and district leaders need knowledge about why teachers leave and how they can retain special educators.

SCENARIO: TWO PERSPECTIVES ON ATTRITION

Principal's Perspective

Ennis Jackson, a principal at Byrd Lincoln Middle School, shakes his head as Isabel Polk leaves his office. He cannot believe she resigned after only three short years—and after all of the energy and time devoted to mentoring her! Isabel showed so much promise, and as a teacher of color, she brought diversity to the special education faculty. She spent the last three years establishing positive relationships with general educators, and developed a new coteaching program with the science teachers. Now a new teacher will have to start over. Ennis wonders if they will ever have any stability in special education. He picks up the phone to call Margaret, the director of special education.

Special Educator's Perspective

As Isabel leaves the principal's office, she has mixed feelings about her resignation. She can tell Ennis is upset. She enjoys the school in many ways, but this job was not what she expected! She needed more support from other teachers and Ennis. The coteaching program had promise, but there were still so many problems. After three years, some of the general educators were still reluctant to collaborate and many days she still felt like an outsider. She was no longer sure what her role was supposed to be anymore—it was frustrating. Her caseload grew from 23 to 28 this year, and the paperwork was overwhelming. She coordinated all referrals and was responsible for all eligibility and Individualized Education Program (IEP) meetings. Isabel felt some of her students were not getting the assistance they deserved. She was not sure anyone could do this job well. With a second child coming, it made sense to stay home for a year or two and think about her options.

Attrition in the Context of Teacher Shortage

Leaders in many districts struggle to find and keep highly qualified special educators. Three major factors contribute to the increasing shortage of special educators:

1. The population of students with disabilities has grown three times faster than the general population of students over the last decade.

2. There are insufficient new graduates of special education programs and former teachers returning to meet the demand.

3. High attrition contributes to additional vacancies (McLeskey et al., 2004).

A shortage of teachers of students with emotional/behavioral disorders is higher than all other special education teaching areas and is a considerable problem in ten of the eleven regions of the United States (American Association for Employment in Education [AAEE], 2000). Other special education teaching areas that are on the "considerable shortage" list include multicategorical, severe/profound disabilities, learning disabilities, mild/moderate disabilities, mental retardation, visually impaired, hearing impaired, and dual certificate (general/special). Only early childhood special education was on the "some shortage" list (AAEE, 2000).

Teacher Shortage in Urban, Rural, and High-Poverty Schools

The teacher shortage is particularly excessive in high-poverty urban schools due to fewer resources and poorer working conditions (Darling-Hammond, 2003). Not only do high-poverty schools have a more difficult time attracting teachers, they have a harder time retaining them (Ingersoll, 2001). According to a study of the largest urban school districts, nearly 98% of those that responded indicated an immediate need for special educators (Silent Crisis, 2004). In one large urban city, 100 long-term substitutes had to be hired to fill vacant special education positions, and when special educators were hired, 40 to 50% left by the end of the third year (Mandlawitz, 2003). Teacher recruitment and retention is also a pressing issue for many rural districts, especially those at a disadvantage because of geography, declining economies, and high rates of poverty (Silent Crisis, 2004; Westling & Whitten, 1996).

The Shortage of Culturally and Linguistically Diverse (CLD) Special Educators

Special educators from culturally and linguistically diverse (CLD) backgrounds are especially difficult to find. In the opening scenario Principal Ennis realizes the importance of having a diverse faculty; however, he may not know about the severe shortages of special educators with CLD backgrounds. Although the student population is becoming more diverse, special educators remain primarily white and female (Billingsley, Carlson, & Klein, 2004; Tyler, Yzquierdo, Lopez-Reyna, & Flippin, 2004). Future projections suggest even greater shortages of teachers from CLD backgrounds.

CHAPTER OVERVIEW

The above scenario is all too typical in many school districts today. Why do so many special education teachers leave each year? For some districts, the serious shortage of qualified special educators makes each teacher resignation a significant loss to the school and district. This chapter addresses:

- The range of factors that contribute to special education teacher attrition,
- Special educators' plans to leave, and,
- Why attrition matters.

WHY SPECIAL EDUCATORS LEAVE

What keeps some special educators in teaching while others give up? Decisions to leave special education fall into two major categories: (1) those due to work, and (2) those that are personal. Figure 2.1 summarizes the research findings on special education teacher attrition and retention over the last decade. The figure shows the broad range of factors linked to special education teacher attrition and retention. In this section, key themes from the research on special education teacher attrition are reviewed.

Personal Circumstances

Teachers sometimes leave because of a spouse's transfer, a new career interest, or a desire to stay home with children. Probably more often, both work and nonwork factors weigh into teachers' decisions to leave or stay. For example, in the first scenario in this chapter, Isabel had difficulty deciding whether to continue teaching after her second child was born. Because Isabel had a particularly difficult teaching year and felt others were unsupportive of her efforts, she decided to resign and stay out of teaching for a while. In Isabel's case, her personal circumstances and work conditions contributed to her decision to leave.

Figure 2.1   Special Education Attrition and Retention Research

Attrition Factors	Primary Findings	Author(s) and Year
Teacher Characteristics and Personal Reasons		
Age	Younger special educators more likely to leave than older teachers	Boe et al. (1997) Cross & Billingsley (1994) Miller et al. (1999) Singer (1992)
Gender	Mixed findings with no consistent relationships across studies	Boe et al. (1997) Miller et al. (1999) Singer (1992)
Personal reasons	Personal reasons unrelated to work contribute to special education attrition (e.g., family move, child rearing, illness, retirement)	Billingsley et al. (1993) Billingsley et al. (1995) Kaff (2004) Morvant et al. (1995)
Teacher Qualifications		
Certification	Higher levels of attrition occur among uncertified than certified teachers.	Miller et al. (1999) Boe et al. (1997)
NTE scores	Teachers with high NTE scores were twice as likely to leave than those with lower scores.	Singer (1992)
Experience	Less experienced teachers are more likely to leave than their experienced colleagues.	Billingsley & Cross, 1992 Miller et al. (1999) Singh & Billingsley (1996)
Work Conditions		
Salary	Teachers with lower salaries were more likely to leave than those with higher salaries.	Boe et al. (1997) Miller et al. (1999) Singer (1992)
Job match	Teachers change jobs to find a better match (e.g., students taught, type of service-delivery, philosophy of program).	Morvant et al. (1995)
Induction	Special educators reporting less effective mentoring are more likely to indicate intent to leave.	Whitaker (2000a)
School climate	Teachers reporting poorer school climates are less likely to stay than those with positive school climates.	Billingsley et al. (2004) Miller et al. (2001)
Administrative support	Inadequate administrative support is linked to more role problems, less job satisfaction, increased stress, lower levels of commitment, and fewer professional development opportunities; lack of administrative support is a major reason given by special educators for leaving their jobs.	Billingsley et al. (1993) Billingsley et al. (1995) Cross & Billingsley (1994) Gersten et al. (2001) Morvant et al. (1995) Singh & Billingsley (1996) Westling & Whitten (1996)

Figure 2.1 (Continued)

Attrition Factors	Primary Findings	Author(s) and Year
Colleague support	Teachers reporting lower levels of colleague support are more likely to leave than those experiencing greater support; inadequate colleague support is related to decisions to leave special education teaching.	Gersten et al. (2001) Miller et al. (1999) Morvant et al. (1995)
Professional development	Teachers reporting less professional development support were less likely to remain in teaching.	Gersten et al. (2001)
Teacher roles	Problems with role overload, conflict, ambiguity, and manageability are associated with attrition; excessive paperwork and meetings (and lack of time for teaching) are contributors to decisions to leave teaching.	Billingsley et al. (1993) Billingsley et al. (1995) Cross & Billingsley (1994) Gersten et al. (2001) Morvant et al. (1995) Singh & Billingsley (1996) Westling & Whitten (1996)
Caseload	Greater diversity in caseload contributes to attrition; high numbers on caseload and inappropriate placement of students with disabilities contributes to attrition.	Billingsley et al. (1993) Billingsley et al. (1995) Brownell et al. (1994-1995) Morvant et al. (1995) Schnorr (1995)
Isolation	Problems with isolation, feeling misunderstood, and not being valued by principals and colleagues contributes to attrition.	Billingsley et al. (1993) George et al. (1995) Morvant et al. (1995)
Service-delivery	Teachers of students with speech, hearing, vision impairments, and emotional disorders are the most likely to leave; teachers in secondary schools more likely to leave than those in elementary schools.	Singer (1992)
Resources	Inadequate resources contribute to attrition.	Billingsley et al. (1993) Billingsley et al. (1995) Morvant et al. (1995)
Teachers' Affective Reactions to Work		
Stress	Teachers reporting higher levels of stress are more likely to leave special education teaching than those reporting lower levels of stress.	Cross & Billingsley (1994) Gersten et al. (2001) Miller et al. (1999) Singh & Billingsley (1996)
Job satisfaction	Special educators who are dissatisfied with their jobs are more likely to leave than those who are more satisfied.	Brownell, Smith, et al. (1997) Cross & Billingsley (1994) Gersten et al. (2001) Singh & Billingsley (1996)
Commitment	Teachers with lower levels of commitment are more likely to leave teaching than those with higher levels of commitment.	Cross & Billingsley (1994) Gersten et al. (2001) Miller et al. (2001)

Teachers may stay for personal reasons. For example, one reason Marie stays in teaching is that her work schedule is compatible with her family responsibilities. Alfonso would like to leave his position, but decides to stay since he is the sole "breadwinner" and cannot find a better position as close to his home.

Problems Adjusting in the First Teaching Years

New special educators are at high risk of leaving (Boe, Bobbitt, Cook, Whitener, & Weber, 1997; Miller et al., 1999). Unfortunately, many eager beginning teachers leave because teaching is not what they hoped it would be. Stress, disillusionment, and burnout in the first teaching years lead to attrition. Recruiting special education teachers will not solve the teacher shortage problem if half leave after the first several years. Envision this loss as a bucket that quickly loses water because of holes in the bottom. Pouring more water in the bucket is a wasted endeavor if we do not first patch the holes (Ingersoll & Smith, 2003).

Lack of Preparation

Special educators without certification are at high risk of leaving (Miller et al., 1999). Unfortunately, many beginning special education teachers do not hold full certification for their main assignments. A recent study reports that over one-third of first-year special educators are not fully qualified for their positions (Billingsley, 2002).

Teachers with minimal qualifications are unfamiliar with best practices, and often are unsure what they do and do not know. Leaders who hire unprepared teachers need to realize that these teachers are at high-risk of leaving, which perpetuates the endless hiring-attrition-recruiting-hiring cycle.

Multiple, Interacting Work Problems

Many special educators leave their positions because of poor work conditions. Figure 2.1 highlights work factors that contribute to attrition, including low salaries, poor job match, isolation, inadequate induction, lack of support, and problems with overwhelming workloads.

While Figure 2.1 shows specific factors that contribute to job dissatisfaction and stress, special educators' reasons for leaving are rarely due to a single work problem; rather, they leave because of multiple, interacting problems (Billingsley, Pyecha, Smith-Davis, Murray, & Hendricks, 1995). For example, Isabel, who began her career well prepared and excited about her work, left after only three years. She lacked both the resources and the support to do her job. She cited the high numbers of students on her caseload, paperwork, administrative duties, and problems working with general educators as reasons for leaving the profession.

Major Problems Experienced by Special Educators

- High caseloads
- Excessive paperwork
- Inadequate planning time (individual and with colleagues)
- Inadequate leadership support
- Teacher isolation
- Insufficient focus on student learning
- Lack of instructional and technological resources

SOURCE: From Kozleski, E., Mainzer, R., & Deshler, D. (2000). Special Education Teaching Conditions Initiative. *Bright Futures for Exceptional Learners: An Action Agenda to Achieve Quality Conditions for Teaching and Learning.* Council for Exceptional Children.

Like Isabel, most special educators enter the field because they want to make a difference in their students' lives. They expect reasonable work conditions, the support of their colleagues and leaders, and for their students to achieve their goals. Teachers need to feel that they have "reached" their students (Johnson & Birkeland, 2003a) and their career decisions are closely tied to whether they succeed. Understanding how work conditions contribute to attrition helps leaders alter the work environment and address problematic areas.

Isolation and Lack of Support

Special educators frequently report feeling only "tolerated" by their principals and colleagues (Kozleski, Mainzer, & Deshler, 2000). Special educators are a minority in public schools and others may not understand their roles or practices. Special educators report that principals and colleagues do not understand the challenges they face nor do they recognize their accomplishments. Special educators hear comments such as, "It must be nice having so few students," or "I don't think it is appropriate to modify the student's exam." Sometimes special educators feel caught between legal requirements and the views of what others see as appropriate.

What Principals Need to Know About Special Education

Jean B. Crockett*

Effective principals are essential to supporting the delivery of high-quality special education. Guided by the requirements of the *Individuals with Disabilities Education Act* (IDEA), special education has an instructional mission and school systems have the legal responsibility to make sure that students with disabilities are provided with what they need to learn. Smart principals also ensure that special educators receive the support needed to do their jobs. Special educators have the responsibility to offer instruction that is highly individualized, intensive, and goal directed. If students with disabilities were no different from typically developing youngsters, there would be no need for special education. But justice has not been blind to the challenges posed by disabilities, nor to the challenges faced by educators in providing what the law requires: a *free appropriate public education* to students with exceptional learning needs. For this reason, special education teachers are expected to have expertise in the following areas: (a) academic instruction of students with learning problems, (b) management of serious behavior problems, (c) use of technological advances, and (d) knowledge of special education law.

Special education is part of the comprehensive educational system in the United States and professional educators share the responsibility for educating all students. The challenge comes in deciding when to differentiate curriculum and instruction and in deciding how to provide students with individual consideration in ways that build on their strengths and strengthen their weaknesses. The IDEA requires school systems to be proactive in identifying children who might have disabilities and in evaluating their eligibility to receive special education, or what the law calls *specially designed instruction*. Each special education student is to be educated to a standard of personal *appropriateness* through an individualized education program (IEP) that addresses his or her unique educational needs. Special education has a tradition of using teams of professionals and parents to make decisions about effective programming for individual students. In this way, the work of special educators can be described as being team based and child centered.

Five Principles of Special Education Leadership

Administrators can better support high-quality programming when they understand what special education is all about and what their roles are in providing its delivery. The following model emphasizes five principles for special education leadership. Each principle is linked to the conceptual foundations of special education addressing ethical practices and moral tensions, individuality and exceptionality, equity under law, effective programming, and productive partnerships (Crockett, 1999-2000).

1. Ethical Practice: Ensuring educational access and accountability for all students. This first principle encourages moral leaders to analyze complexities, respect others, and advocate for child-benefit, justice, and full educational opportunity for every learner. The principle of *Ethical Practice* prompts leaders to consider how they are ensuring educational access and accountability in their classrooms, schools, and communities for a diversity of students, including students with disabilities.

2. Individual Consideration: Addressing individuality and exceptionality in learning. This second principle encourages leaders to be attentive to the relationship between the unique learning and behavioral needs of students with disabilities and specially designed instruction to address their educational progress. The principle of *Individual Consideration* prompts leaders to question if their programs are considerate of students' specific learning needs, and sensitive to exceptional differences that might handicap a child's future if unobserved or left untended. Providing specially designed instruction, different in kind from that provided to other students, requires vigilance to principles of fairness and adherence to procedural safeguards.

3. Equity Under Law: Providing an appropriate education through equitable public policies. This third principle encourages leaders to commit themselves to implementing disability law and fiscal policies that provide special education students with a free appropriate public education. The principle requiring *Equity Under Law* prompts leaders to examine their compliance with federal legislation such as the IDEA, *Section 504* of the *Rehabilitation Act of 1973*, and the *Americans with Disabilities Act* (ADA). This principle asks leaders to inspect their policies and practices to ensure that special education students receive an appropriate education through IEPs designed to provide not just access to the general curriculum, but to educational benefit. To ensure that a student's educational benefits are accruing, leaders are challenged to monitor individual outcomes closely.

4. Effective Programming: Providing individualized programming designed to enhance student performance. This fourth principle encourages leaders to foster high expectations, support research-based strategies, and target positive results for special education students. The principle of *Effective Programming* prompts leaders to support teachers in linking instructional strategies with what a student needs to learn and how he or she needs to learn it. Special emphasis should be placed on providing instruction in ways that address students' disability-related needs and ensure them with access to appropriate learning opportunities within and beyond the general education curriculum.

5. Productive Partnerships: Establishing relationships that foster learning. This fifth principle encourages leaders to communicate, negotiate, and collaborate with others on behalf of students with disabilities and their families. Educating diverse learners is a complex task. The principle of *Productive Partnerships* prompts leaders to question how well the members of their own learning communities collaborate and how effectively they partner with parents and service agencies in responding to the needs of vulnerable youth and families.

Every core principle can be described as interacting with each of the others to form a constellation of factors to consider in providing high-quality special education. The principle of *Equity Under Law* intersects with each principle in a special way by protecting students who might otherwise suffer discrimination if their differences were merely celebrated but not addressed. In an ideal world, the other four principles—*Ethical Practice, Individual Consideration, Effective Programming,* and *Productive Partnerships*—if implemented fully and in good faith, might well serve the education of all students. As a model for supporting high-quality special education, however, the *Principles for Special Education Leadership* acknowledge the significance of the IDEA and reinforce the concept that special education is an integral part of American schooling and not a legal event.

---

*Jean B. Crockett, PhD, is an associate professor of Special Education Administration and Supervision, Virginia Tech Department of Educational Leadership and Policy Studies.

Special educators also report feeling devalued. As one teacher states:

I was so surprised at the comments from the general education teachers. One teacher actually asked me if I had to complete a 4-year degree like a regular teacher in order to teach "those" students. She made it sound like I wasn't bright enough to be a "real" teacher—I have a master's degree! Another teacher told me I didn't deserve to make the same salary as her since I had fewer students and my lesson plans were so easy because I didn't teach "real skills." (*Addressing the Revolving Door, How to Retain Your Special Education Teachers,* 2004)

Special educators are often the last to receive resources. An itinerant teacher stated:

The principal was very reluctant to give me anything and seemed to be reluctant to treat me as a staff member. Her teachers were allotted certain materials and I was not. . . . Practically the first thing out of her mouth was: "Well, whose budget are you on?" I guess she epitomized the whole thing when, on the very last day of school, she mispronounced my name. That kind of epitomized the whole year. (Gersten, Gillman, Morvant, & Billingsley, 1995, pp. 4–5)

Some special educators indicate they are unwelcome as they work with general educators to include students with disabilities. In some inclusive settings, special educators report feeling like outsiders, or as assistants or aides, rather than professionals (Embich, 2001). Others report that they encounter feelings of hostility. As one teacher stated, "The school staff for the most part, resents the accommodations which they are asked to make for special needs students" (Kozleski et al., 2000 p. 5). Lack of support from administrators and colleagues often leads to feelings of isolation, alienation, and a poor school climate for special educators.

Role Problems

Many special educators struggle with changing teacher roles as they move to environments that are more inclusive. Special educators experience numerous role problems that include role ambiguity (lacking necessary information to do their work), role conflict (being asked to do contradictory things), and role overload (having more to do than is reasonable). Special educators particularly feel torn between the teaching tasks they know are critical and the burdensome paperwork and meetings that demand their time (Billingsley, 2004). Some special educators spend up to a day and a half per week on paperwork (Kozleski et al., 2000). Although all teachers experience some role issues, prolonged difficulties lead to chronic stress and burnout.

Stress and Burnout

Some special educators work in environments that make it difficult, if not impossible, to do their work well. Some suggest that burnout is the most important element in a teacher's desire to quit. Almost 40% of special educators who moved to general education teaching indicated "burnout" was the primary factor (Billingsley & Cross, 1991). Teachers who report "burnout" often have increased absences from work, think about quitting, and begin to search for new jobs. Special educators have many choices—someone else will hire them.

SPECIAL EDUCATORS' PLANS TO LEAVE

Approximately half of the special education attrition research studies identified in Figure 2.1 addressed teachers' *plans to leave* teaching, not actual attrition. Although controversial as a measure of attrition, studying plans to leave provides an understanding of teachers' career intentions without the time-consuming task of finding those who left (Billingsley, 2004). Indeed, plans to leave predict actual leaving (Gersten et al., 2001). Studying special educators' career plans can provide school and district leaders with a sense of how many special educators want to leave.

Figure 2.2 highlights the career plans of a large national sample of special educators. Approximately 20% are undecided regarding how long they plan to stay, and 6% plan to leave as soon as possible. How long these undecided teachers stay will have an important impact on future shortages (*Recruiting and Retaining High-Quality Teachers*, 2002).

Some teachers who want to leave stay for years. Although physically present, these teachers often disengage, leaving energy for new learning, supporting others, and trying new approaches to teaching. Often the lack of effort leads to ineffective practice, thus reducing students' opportunities to learn.

WHY ATTRITION MATTERS

The attrition of special educators wastes critically needed talent. High levels of attrition are costly, reduce teacher quality, divert attention from school improvement efforts, and interfere with the quality of services that

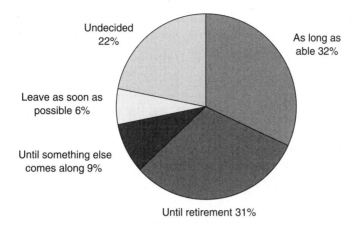

Figure 2.2   Special Educators' Plans to Remain in Teaching

SOURCE: From *Recruiting and Retaining High-Quality Teachers*, 2002.

students with disabilities receive. Teachers, students, administrators, and taxpayers all bear the costs of attrition. School and district leaders who understand the factors that contribute to attrition can address the challenge of improving retention.

Teacher Quality

Researchers and policy makers agree that highly qualified teachers make a difference in student achievement (Darling-Hammond & Youngs, 2002). When qualified special educators leave, they are often replaced by individuals with less experience, and quite possibly without full qualifications to teach students with disabilities.

Districts who hire unqualified teachers also expose students to a "continual parade of ineffective teachers" (Darling-Hammond, 2003, p. 9), since these teachers often leave before they become skilled. In the meantime, significant resources are required to help new special educators acquire needed knowledge and teaching skills.

Even if a qualified teacher is hired, it usually takes a while for the new teacher to apply what he or she has learned to the real world of teaching. These teachers not only have full teaching responsibilities, but they are still learning to teach. Reducing the number of years students receive instruction from novices should help improve educational quality (Darling-Hammond, 2003).

School Improvement

High levels of attrition also interfere with workforce stability (Hope, 1999). For example, incorporating research-based practices requires the professional development of faculty as well as sustained efforts to integrate new skills into daily practice. Frequent staff changes interfere with these ongoing efforts and new teachers are unlikely to pick up where others left off. Collaborative relationships between general and special educators also take time to develop, and frequent turnover disrupts these relationships. Principal Ennis knows that the coteaching program Isabel helped establish depends on the collaborative relationships Isabel established with other teachers.

School and district leaders may resort to undesirable program practices when qualified special educators are not available, such as reducing services to students with disabilities or raising teachers' caseloads (Billingsley, 1993). These actions may actually contribute to attrition since overburdened teachers experience more stress.

Costs of Attrition

It is costly to replace teachers. Districts spend thousands of dollars for every teacher leaving the district in separation, hiring, and induction costs (Benner, 2000). A more stable special education workforce allows these resources to be devoted to other school and district needs.

CHAPTER SUMMARY

- Efforts to increase teacher retention should be a priority for school and district leaders since attrition is a major contributor to the shortage of special educators.
- Teachers who leave because of work factors usually report multiple, interacting work problems, including lack of support, isolation, teacher role problems (e.g., changing roles, role overload, stress).
- Understanding what contributes to attrition provides leaders with an opportunity to improve special educators' work conditions.
- High attrition rates are costly to school districts, interfere with educational programs, and reduce students' with disabilities opportunities to learn.
- Two groups of teachers are at high risk of leaving: new teachers and uncertified teachers.

SELECTED READINGS

Billingsley, B. (2004). Special education teacher retention and attrition: A critical analysis of the research literature. *The Journal of Special Education*, *38*(1), 39–55.

Brownell, M., Hirsch, E., Seo, S. (2004). Meeting the demand for highly qualified special education teachers during severe shortages: What should policymakers consider? *The Journal of Special Education, 38*(1), 22–38.

Gersten, R., Keating T., Yovanoff, P., & Harniss, M. K. (2001). Working in special education: Factors that enhance special educators' intent to stay. *Exceptional Children, 6*(4), 549–567.

Kozleski, E., Mainzer, R., & Deshler, D. (2000) Special Education Teaching Conditions Initiative. *Bright Futures for Exceptional Learners*—Introduction: *An Action Agenda to Achieve Quality Conditions for Teaching and Learning.* Council for Exceptional Children. http://www.cec.sped.org/spotlight/cond/bf_intro.html

McLeskey, J., Tyler, N., & Flippin, S. S. (2004). The supply of and demand for special education teachers: A review of research regarding the nature of the chronic shortage of special education teachers. *The Journal of Special Education, 38*(1), 5–22.

Tyler, N., Yzquierdo, Z., Lopez-Reyna, N., & Flippin, S. S. (2004). Cultural and linguistic diversity and the special education workforce: A critical overview. *The Journal of Special Education, 38*(1), 22–38.

WEB SITES

Addressing the Revolving Door: How to Retain Your Special Education Teachers (Star Legacy Module)

http://iris.peabody.vanderbilt.edu/retention/chalcycle.htm

This online module is an introduction to special education teacher attrition and includes a summary of the research, interviews, readings, and supplementary activities.

Center of Personnel Studies in Special Education (COPSSE)

http://www.coe.ufl.edu/copsse/index.php

Provides research briefs and syntheses related to teacher supply and demand, the effectiveness of professional preparation, and certification and licensure.

National Clearinghouse for Professions in Special Education (NCPSE)

http://www.special-ed-careers.org/about_us/index.html

Provides information regarding special education personnel preparation, recruitment, and retention. NCPSE collects, organizes, and disseminates information regarding personnel needs. The NCPSE Web site features a range of reports and useful documents, such as its recruitment toolkit: http://www.special-ed-careers.org/research_library/recruitment_kit.html

Study of Personnel Needs in Special Education (SPeNSE)

http://ferdig.coe.ufl.edu/spense/

A range of reports provide information about work conditions, state and local policies, professional development, beginning special educators, and special educator recruitment and retention.

Part II

Finding and Cultivating High-Quality Special Educators

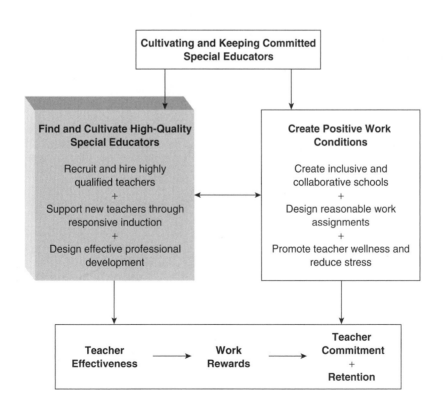

Recruiting and Hiring Highly Qualified Special Educators

3

Help Wanted: Individuals who are enthusiastic, intelligent, energetic, and personable to work in challenging situations with challenging individuals. Extrinsic rewards minimal. Intrinsic rewards unlimited.

(Mastropieri, 2001, p. 66)

S pecial education teachers are difficult to find. Each year thousands of special education positions are left vacant or filled with teachers who are not fully qualified. Although some states hire few uncertified teachers, others report that up to 32% of their special education teachers are not fully certified for their main assignments (McLeskey et al., 2004).

Obviously, the shallow pool of special educators is a major barrier to hiring highly qualified teachers. Other barriers include insufficient salaries and benefits, late job postings, and the geographic locations of the schools (Recruiting and Retaining High-Quality Teachers, 2002).

Recruiting and hiring qualified special education teachers will continue to be a major challenge for busy administrators given the shortage of special educators and the requirements of the NCLB Act. However, making the most of the recruiting and hiring processes has important payoffs—highly qualified teachers will not only be more effective teachers of students with disabilities—they also are more likely to stay, thereby reducing turnover and providing continuity.

Special Education Qualifications and NCLB

Schools will need to meet the teacher personnel requirements of the NCLB Act when making hiring decisions by the 2005-2006 school year, with some additional flexibility for rural districts. The NCLB Act outlines the minimum requirements that highly qualified teachers must meet. However, the law provides flexibility for states to develop their own definition of "highly qualified" that is consistent with the NCLB Act as well as the unique needs of each state (NCLB, 2002). To meet the NCLB Act requirements, a highly qualified teacher must have:

1. a bachelor's degree,

2. full state certification and licensure as defined by the state, and

3. demonstrated competency, as defined by the state, in each core academic subject taught.

The state has the freedom to define certification, streamline its certification process, and create alternate routes to certification. States are provided with significant flexibility, especially for core academic teachers with experience. For example, the "high objective uniform State standard of evaluation" (HOUSSE) allows experienced teachers to demonstrate subject-matter competency that recognizes experience, expertise, and professional training earned over time (for more information, see NCLB Act Section 9101[(23]).

Special education teachers must meet the highly qualified teacher requirements for any core subjects that they teach, regardless of the setting in which they work. However, special educators who do not provide direct instruction and only consult with teachers of core subjects are not required to be highly qualified in those content areas ("New No Child Left Behind Flexibility," 2004). Currently, how the highly qualified teacher provisions of the NCLB Act apply to special educators is being reviewed in the context of the Individuals with Disabilities Education Act (IDEA) reauthorization.

SCENARIO: "WHERE ARE THE QUALIFIED APPLICANTS?"

Margaret Parrish, the special education director in the Westover City Schools, shuffles through a pile of teacher applications with Principal

Ennis. Margaret suggests they better move fast if they are to hire these applicants who will no doubt receive other job offers. Margaret considers the 25 new special educators they hired last year. Unfortunately, eight had inadequate preparation, but she didn't have enough qualified applicants. Four of these unqualified teachers already left the district, and one transferred to a middle school English position. This year it seems there are even fewer qualified applicants than last year. Margaret and Ennis want to learn more about how better recruiting and hiring practices can help them find qualified special educators who are a good match for their positions.

CHAPTER OVERVIEW

This chapter provides practical information and resources important to the successful finding and hiring of highly qualified special education teachers. Specifically, the chapter addresses:

- Recruiting special education teachers
- Effective hiring and assignment practices

This chapter also incorporates information to help assess special education teacher qualifications, including information on special education teacher certification, teacher preparation programs, and teacher accreditation programs. Diversity considerations in recruitment and hiring are also addressed. Forms and checklists are also provided to assist with screening and interviewing special education applicants.

RECRUITING SPECIAL EDUCATION TEACHERS

The ability to hire qualified special education teachers in a time of teacher shortage depends on the district's ability to attract qualified applicants. In this section four considerations are outlined for increasing the chances for hiring qualified special education teachers. These include: (1) expanding the applicant pool, (2) recruiting from diverse teacher groups, (3) developing grow-your-own programs, and (4) marketing your special education program.

Expand the Applicant Pool

Most administrators recruit special education teachers by contacting colleges and universities, notifying educators in other schools and agencies, and advertising in local publications. Only about half advertise for special educators in national publications, and large districts are more likely to advertise nationally than smaller and medium sized districts (U.S. Department of Education, 2001). Because of the lack of readily available teachers in special education, districts should consider expanding their recruitment strategies.

Districts should consider moving beyond traditional recruitment methods and include the use of job fairs, external recruiters, and Web sites. For example, electronic bulletin boards allow administrators to list job openings and encourage applicants to apply for positions via the Web (see Figure 3.1). Other districts provide virtual tours of their districts for applicants to view prior to their visit. The electronic system has been extended to other states, and those using it have reported success in recruiting teachers ("Recruiting and Retaining High-Quality Teachers," 2002).

Recruit From Diverse Teacher Groups

Special educators from culturally and/or linguistically diverse (CLD) backgrounds are in short supply. Many school districts report a desperate need for teachers from CLD groups. Schools need teachers who reflect the diversity of their communities, and students with disabilities need role models. For students from CLD backgrounds in special education, a racially and ethnically diverse teaching staff can help foster self-confidence and higher levels of achievement (Tyler et al., 2004).

Have You Considered That Diversifying Your Teaching Faculty:

- Is the equitably correct thing to do?
- May result in fewer inappropriate referrals and placements of students from diverse backgrounds?
- May increase academic achievement for students from diverse backgrounds?
- Can provide closer links between the school, home, and community?
- Can enhance multicultural communication skills of all children?

SOURCE: From *Diversifying the Special Education Workforce: Special Education Workforce Watch* (2004). Center for Personnel Studies in Special Education (No. PB-10), Gainesville, FL: University of Florida.

In special education, the overrepresentation of students from CLD backgrounds suggests an even greater need to attract a diverse special

Name and Address of Web Site	Description of Site
The Council for Exceptional Children http://www.cec.sped.org	Provides information on special education teacher accreditation and a job bank (see CEC Career Connections). School districts can also post job openings.
The National Clearinghouse for Professions in Special Education (NCPSE) http://www.special-ed-careers.org/	The NCPSE provides information related to the recruitment, preparation, and retention of well-qualified diverse special educators.
National Teacher Recruitment Clearinghouse http://www.recruitingteachers.org	This website provides information for teachers seeking positions, suggests strategies for effective teacher recruitment, development, and retention (includes a portal to links to over 800 job banks).
Recruiting New Teachers http://www.rnt.org	Recruiting New Teachers, Inc. (RNT) addresses improving the nation's teacher recruitment, development, and diversity policies and practices. The Web Site provides a job bank and numerous other sources about teacher recruitment and retention.
Educational Placement Services (EPS) http://www.educatorjobs.com/	EPS provides jobs for public and private schools and is one of the largest teacher placement services in the United State
American Association for Employment in Education (AAEE) http://www.ub-careers.buffalo.edu/ aaee/pro_pubs.shtml#RTB	This site lists hundreds of job vacancies for interested teachers and includes resources to help educators with their job search.
JobBank USA http://www.jobbankusa.com/ohb/ohb070. html	This Web Site provides career and employment services to job applicants, employers, and recruiters.
Teachers-Teachers.com http://teachers-teachers.com/	The Web Site is designed to help districts find teachers, administrators, and related services providers.

Figure 3.1   Selected Teacher Recruitment Web Sites

education teaching force (Dooley, 2003). States, universities, colleges, and school districts need to incorporate effective strategies for recruiting teachers from CLD backgrounds. Targeted recruitment efforts are needed to increase the diversity of applicants. Recruiting alternatively certified special educators is one strategy since about 40% of these teachers are from culturally and linguistically diverse backgrounds (see Textbox, pp.38–41). Another consideration is recruiting from Historically Black Colleges and Universities. Almost half of all African American students in undergraduate teacher preparation programs are from historically Black colleges and universities.

What Administrators Should Know About Alternative Certification Programs

*Paul T. Sindelar and Michael S. Rosenberg**

The federal government has encouraged the development of alternative routes to certification noting that such approaches "streamline the process of certification to move candidates into the classroom on a fast-track basis" (U.S. Department of Education, 2002). School administrators may or may not find hope in this strategy for coping with an inadequate supply of highly qualified teachers.

The Department of Education's recommended strategy is based on the idea that student achievement is more closely tied to teachers' subject matter knowledge than to their instructional skills. The department posits that streamlining training requirements will encourage high-ability candidates—individuals who chose to forgo teacher preparation as undergraduates—to enter the profession. Many school and district administrators question the logic of requiring less training for special education teachers. Administrators recognize that, if students with disabilities are to succeed in school, their teachers must master sophisticated and complex instructional techniques, in the social as well as academic domains. They understand that such expertise cannot be attained without extensive supervised practice.

But administrators also know that undertaking a traditional, campus-based teacher preparation program is no guarantee that trainees will get "extensive supervised practice," either. Being pragmatic, administrators seek competent and motivated teachers, regardless of how they were prepared. They recognize that the division that separates adequate from inadequate preparation is not always the same line that divides traditional from alternative routes. And, because many school districts are themselves preparing teachers, administrators are increasingly faced with the question of what makes training programs effective.

The professional literature offers some guidance. Successful alternative routes are not the shortcut routes envisioned by advocates of the NCLB Act. To the contrary, in research on special education alternative routes, successful programs have proven lengthy and rigorous. Their planning and implementation typically involved extensive collaboration among universities, state departments of education, and districts. Successful programs tended to emphasize field experiences, and supervision was shared by district and university mentors.

The number of programs on which we based these findings was small, a fact that tempers our confidence in the generality of the conclusions. Moreover, the programs described in the professional literature are not likely to represent alternative route programs generally. (Because university faculty are expected to publish their work, programs offered or cosponsored by universities are likely to be overrepresented in published research.) As a result, we have turned to other kinds of analyses to generate meaningful guidelines for the development and implementation of alternative routes, most notably economic analysis.

We have worked with economists at the University of Florida's Bureau of Economic and Business Research to develop both a model of the cost effectiveness of training options and guidelines for developing successful alternative routes. Cost is important because states and districts have limited funds for training and because they bear the responsibility of simultaneously increasing the supply of teachers and improving teacher quality. Teacher retention plays a critical role in the model, so that programs whose graduates enter and remain in the field will be more cost effective than programs whose graduates leave sooner or in greater numbers. For example, some research has shown that 5-year programs are more cost effective in the long term than less expensive programs because their graduates remain in teaching longer. Our analysis also suggests that new programs must be required to supplement the supply of teachers. New programs that serve candidates who would have availed themselves of other preparation options add nothing to supply. Such programs cannibalize existing programs and drive up costs.

The Human Capital Theory (HCT), our economist colleagues have explained, offers useful insights about program development and, more particularly, about candidate selection and program requirements. Candidates who bring more human capital to special education teaching, they say, are more likely to remain in the field than candidates who bring less. Thus, people who worked in occupations like teaching are more likely to persist in teaching than people who worked in quite different jobs. Similarly, people who reside in a community are more likely to persist in a school in that community than outsiders.

In fact, people who worked in a particular building were more likely to remain in that building than were people from elsewhere.

Our colleagues are especially optimistic about the potential of paraprofessional step-up programs, because participants in such programs bring much human capital to their work. After all, they have worked in schools and with children, and presumably have demonstrated an aptitude for such work. They are likely to live in the communities and schools where they work and are trained, and are likely to remain there once they become teachers. By contrast, mid-career changers—the scientists and mathematicians that the U. S. Department of Education expects alternative route programs to attract—represent a riskier clientele. For one thing, most must take a pay cut to enter teaching—often forgoing hundreds of thousands of dollars in lifetime earnings; for another, the jobs they are leaving may be quite unlike teaching, meaning they bring less occupation specific human capital to their new profession. Moreover, mid-career changers are less likely to live in communities with hard-to-staff schools and so are less likely to persist in areas where they're needed most.

This analysis does not imply that programs for mid-career changers are necessarily inferior to programs for paraprofessionals. They do suggest that program administrators take more caution in selecting program participants. After all, school administrators are likely to know far less about the potential of mid-career changers than about the paraprofessionals they currently employ. Furthermore, some mid-career changers are better bets to complete training and persist in teaching than others. It behooves trainers to identify and select mid-career changers with better potential for persistence and success.

The HCT also suggests that individuals who invest more in their own training are more likely to persist in the field. This strategy is pertinent to programs for mid-career changers, because we know less about the seriousness of their intent, their ease with children, or their aptitude for teaching. In this sense, fast-track programs present a problem: Because they do not require substantial investment of time and energy, shortcut programs are unlikely to discourage participants who are indifferent to the field. By contrast, increasing the rigor of program requirements may dissuade the incompetent and unmotivated without discouraging strong candidates.

Administrators are ultimately responsible for providing highly qualified teachers for all students, including students with disabilities, and history has proven that that is no easy task. Although alternatives to traditional teacher preparation offer hope of increasing the supply of teachers, we know that not all alternative routes are created equal. As a colleague of ours has aptly put it, "There are alternative routes, *and there are alternative routes . . ."*

---

*Dr. Paul T. Sindelar is a professor in special education at the University of Florida. He is also director of the Center for Personnel Studies in Special Education (COPSSE). See www.copsse.org.

Dr. Michael S. Rosenberg is a professor in special education at Johns Hopkins University.

Consider "Grow Your Own" Programs

"Grow your own" programs prepare local individuals who are already working in schools, local graduates with little or no postsecondary education, or mid-career individuals looking for a career change. For example, developing an on-site teacher preparation program or paying tuition for qualified paraprofessionals or substitute teachers to earn a special education teaching degree can increase the pool of available teachers in the district. "Growyourown" programs also allow the content of teacher preparation to be adapted to local needs and circumstances ("Enlarging the Pool," 2003). Individuals with particular characteristics can also be recruited, such as bilingual individuals and those from diverse groups.

Given that many new hires accept positions close to home (Billingsley, 2002), finding prospective teachers in your own community makes sense. Individuals from the community are also in a position to understand the community and may be better able to relate with parents than those teachers who are brought in from the outside ("Enlarging the Pool," 2003).

Some districts develop high school programs to interest local individuals in educational careers. An example is the "Cadet Teacher Academy," which provides opportunities for students in high schools to develop an understanding of teaching careers and opportunities (see the South Carolina teacher cadet program http://www.cerra.org/).

Market Your Special Education Program

A range of strategies can be used by the district to market the special education program, such as promotional materials (e.g., high-quality brochures), job fairs, university departments of education, and placement fairs. For an example of a promotional brochure, see The National Clearinghouse for the Professions Web site at http://www.special-ed-careers.org. Also, administrators should consider advertising positions on Web sites with special education job banks (see Figure 3.1).

Administrators should be sure to highlight the strengths of their school and district. Applicants desire a strong compensation package, the best possible working conditions, supportive principals and colleagues, and access to materials and resources. Providing a well-developed induction program is also a positive recruitment tool.

Offer Special Incentives

Districts sometimes offer special incentives to recruit teachers. In one study, only 15% of local administrators offered local special financial incentives to recruit special education teachers, and larger districts were more likely to provide these incentives than smaller ones ("Recruiting and Retaining High-Quality Teachers," 2002). More districts will likely begin offering incentives as they become more desperate for teachers. Districts can offer a range of incentives when making an offer. Financial incentives include:

- Signing bonuses (which vary from $1,000 to $20,000);
- Salary advances;
- Assistance with acquiring homes (e.g., low downpayments on homes; paying closing costs; low-rate mortgages; counseling on home buying);
- Paying for coursework to earn certification in special education;
- Student loan repayment; and
- Bonuses for teaching in critical demand areas or schools.

Other incentives include:

- Principal and staff who are knowledgeable about and interested in providing strong programs for students with disabilities;
- Strong induction and mentor programs;
- Professional development opportunities (e.g., attending a professional conference);
- Grants to cover professional development costs;
- Reasonable teaching materials budget;
- Job sharing; and
- Reduced responsibilities during the first year.

EFFECTIVE HIRING AND ASSIGNMENT PRACTICES

Strong leaders know that one of their most important responsibilities is hiring the best teachers they can find. However, finding highly qualified teachers is easier for some districts and schools than others. School leaders who are systematic in their hiring process, offer competitive compensation packages, and provide good working conditions will find it easier to recruit and keep committed special educators. Districts that begin hiring early also have an advantage over those that wait until the late weeks of summer.

Evaluating whether special education teachers are "highly qualified" or a good match for a particular position may be daunting to principals, who often have questions about special education certification and the desirable attributes of applicants (see Textbox, this page). The more the principal understands about special education and how it operates in the school and the district, the easier it will be to evaluate applicants' credentials and respond to their questions. Applicants are also more attracted to schools where principals are involved in, knowledgeable about, and committed to strong special education programs.

Understanding Special Education Certification

There is no area of education licensure with as much variability as special education (Mainzer & Horvath, 2001). Special education certification encompasses a range of categories and terms such as, learning disabilities, visual impairments, orthopedic impairments, speech/language impairments, emotional disturbance, behavioral disorders, and mental retardation.

Categorical and Noncategorical Certification

There are two major approaches to state certification in special education, "categorical, and "noncategorical." The majority of states issue categorical special education credentials; seven do not. In categorical systems, special education teachers are licensed to teach children who have been identified with particular disabilities. For example, Raoul, a special educator, has a state endorsement to teach only students with emotional disorders.

In contrast, some states have noncategorical or multicategorical certification, in which special educators typically teach students across two or more disability groups. For example, Lauren holds a mild/moderate certification allowing her to teach students with behavioral disorders, specific learning disabilities, mild mental retardation, and other health impairments. A severe/profound certification is geared toward teaching students with mental retardation and multiple disabilities.

Most states include expansive age/grade ranges for special education certification. The majority of states include grades 1 through 12 in special education certification, allowing teachers to work at any school level. The most common reported age range for licensing early childhood special educators is birth through five years (Geiger, Crutchfield, & Mainzer, 2003).

Alternative Certification

Alternative certification programs have grown in many states in response to the special education teacher shortage (McLeskey et al., 2004; Rosenberg & Sindelar, 2001). The proliferation of alternative programs will likely expand given the requirements of the NCLB Act. Although alternatively certified teachers are usually required to meet the same standards as graduates of traditional programs (Geiger et al., 2003), their program requirements often look very different. For example, those teachers finishing alternative programs were more likely to take summer courses and seminars, rather than traditional courses, and fieldwork was completed while the participants were teachers, rather than during an internship. Supervision also tends to be provided by mentor teachers rather than university faculty (see Textbox 3.3 for more on alternative certification).

Advanced Certification

Today an advanced certification from The National Board for Professional Teaching Standards (NBPTS) is available to encourage the development of highlyskilled teachers who will serve as leaders in schools (another advanced certification, the American Board's certification for Master Teacher, is under development). The NBPTS offers a National Board Certified Teacher (NBCT) designation, which is available to those who hold a baccalaureate degree and have three years of public or private classroom experience. Nearly all who have prepared for the NBCT exam agree that it was rigorous and is the most valuable professional development opportunity that they have experienced ("National Boards Set Standards," 2004).

Some districts give priority to NBCT applicants. For example, some states automatically grant licenses to NBCT teachers who move in to their district or, for those already in the district, count them as Master Teachers. States and districts often offer financial rewards for NBCT-certified teachers, such as yearly stipends ranging from $2,500 to $7,500 for the life of their certificate ("National Boards Set Standards" 2004).

Centralized Versus Decentralized Hiring

School hiring practices may be centralized or decentralized. When hiring is centralized, the district personnel office and the special education administrator complete the major hiring tasks. In this arrangement, the specific characteristics of the teaching positions and the specific needs of particular schools are not considered until the late stages of the process, if at all (Liu, 2003). For example, when Josephine was offered a contract for her special education position, she was told that she would not receive her specific school assignment until school began, and it might be in any elementary school in the district. Josephine did not accept the contract because she wanted to meet the principal, and determine how well the school and the specific assignment matched her expectations for the position.

In contrast, under a more decentralized process, new teachers are hired by individual schools after an initial screening by the district office (Liu, 2003). A decentralized process has advantages for the applicants and school staff which include:

- Tailoring job descriptions to the specific needs of the school and the special education program within the school;
- Evaluating the extent to which the applicant's abilities, experiences, and dispositions match both the position and the culture of the school; and
- Allowing the applicant to develop a more accurate picture of the job (Liu, 2003).

Some districts fall somewhere between highly centralized and decentralized hiring approaches. Special education directors often do an initial screening, which is likely to be preferred by busy principals who would rather focus their energy on interviewing a smaller, more select group of applicants later in the process.

Recruit and Hire Early

Districts should begin the process of recruiting and hiring as soon as possible—it gives administrators the best chance of finding well-qualified teachers who are a good match for their available positions. Hiring early also provides new teachers with the time necessary to set up their classrooms and prepare for the year.

Hiring delays until July or August make it harder to hire qualified teachers (Levin & Quinn, 2003). Levin and Quinn find that applicants committed to working in urban schools withdraw after months in limbo and districts lose their stronger applicants and hire weaker ones. In fact, up to one-third of urban teachers are hired after the school year starts (Liu, 2003).

Identify Desirable Teacher Characteristics

The development of a position or job description is a good start to considering areas of expertise that are needed. Will the special educator be working in a full-time special education or resource classroom or coteaching for most of the day? What specific characteristics and skills does the special education teacher need to have? Chapter 7 provides an example of a role description for a special educator. Be sure to look for applicants who demonstrate a caring attitude toward students and a strong commitment to working with students with disabilities.

Carefully Screen Applicants

If there are few applicants for a position, try to interview most if not all of them. For those fortunate enough to have a larger pool of applicants, a screening process is needed to identify the strongest candidates. Initially, applications should be screened against predetermined criteria, including certification, preparation, experience, tests, and letters of recommendation. Figure 3.2 provides a worksheet for evaluating applicants against these five criteria. These criteria can be adapted to suit the needs of the school and a place is provided at the end of the form for comments. Following this exercise, administrators can rank applicants and contact those with the best qualifications for interviews.

Special Education Certification

If you ask administrators about the criteria they look for when hiring special educators, they will no doubt include state certification. However, administrators may not realize that an added bonus of hiring a certified teacher is that they are more likely to stay than those who are not certified. Be sure to consider whether the teacher has the type and range of certifications needed for the position (see Textbox 3.4 for information about special education certification).

Teacher Preparation

Leaders need to look beyond the credential and ask questions about the applicant's preparation for teaching. When possible, try to hire special educators who have completed strong teacher preparation programs with extensive field requirements. Special education teachers who receive a

Criteria	Applicant Names and Phone Numbers									
	Yes	No	Yes	No	Yes	No	Yes	No	Yes	No
Holds full State certificate for the students and grade levels to be taught										
Holds full State certification in relevant exceptionality area(s)										
Holds an emergency or temporary State certificate endorsement										
Completed a State-approved teacher education program										
Has college major that matches the teaching assignment										
Has relevant experience in teaching area, school level										
Has obtained passing scores for required tests										
Has recommendations from previous employers/supervisors										
Comments:										

Figure 3.2   Special Education Applicant Screening Form

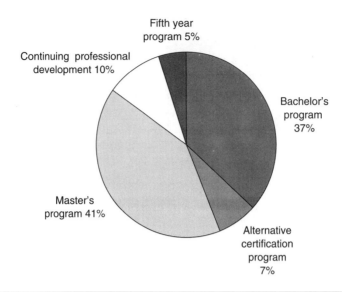

Figure 3.3   Special Education Teachers' Routes to Certification

SOURCE: Carlson, E., Brauen, M., Klein, S., Schroll, K., & Willig, S. (2002). *Key Findings From the Study of Personnel Needs in Special Education.* Bethesda, MD: WESTAT.

high-quality preservice preparation program feel better prepared to handle their job requirements and the diverse student learning needs than those with less preparation ("A High-Quality Teacher for Every Classroom," 2002).

Another consideration is whether the candidate completed a program approved by one of the teacher accreditation councils (i.e., the National Council for Accreditation of Teacher Education [NCATE] or the Teacher Education Accreditation Council [TEAC]). NCATE Special Education Content Standards are made up of ten narrative standards. A four-page summary of these standards is available on the Council for Exceptional Children [CEC] Web site (http://www.cec.sped.org).

Experience

Administrators need to consider the extent and level of experience that applicants have in working with students with disabilities. Ideally, applicants will have extensive experience in settings similar to the one for which they are applying. For new teachers, administrators should consider the length and intensity of their supervised field experience, as well as other related previous experience (e.g., volunteering, work experience as a paraprofessional).

Teacher Tests

Approximately 75% of beginning special educators complete a test for certification that measures academic skills (Billingsley, 2002) such as the

Praxis I exam (Educational Testing Service, 2004). Other Praxis scores may also be required, such as the Praxis II special education specialty tests, which include exams in exceptional education core content as well as a range of specific areas (e.g., learning disabilities, mild to moderate disabilities). Praxis III exams are comprised of direct observation of teaching practice, written testing materials, and semi-structured interviews.

References

Administrators should consider each applicant's references. Do they have letters of recommendation from former employers? If the teacher is a recent graduate, did they include a faculty member from their university program as well as a supervising teacher as references? It is often helpful to followup by calling those who provided written references. Sometimes individuals will be more candid in conversation than in writing.

Make a Good First Impression

Applicants' initial contacts with the school system are important. Some applicants are discouraged by disorganized personnel departments that do not followup with their requests for information, or do not even acknowledge the receipt of an application. There are reports of administrators who indicate that they cannot fill positions, even though highly qualified teachers have applied.

Some teachers are discouraged by their initial contacts from the school system. Shail, a graduate from our teacher preparation program, sent me the following e-mail after attending a job fair:

> The job fair was NOT very impressive—it was pretty disorganized. I was told I was going to interview with an elementary school although I made it really clear in my application packet in three different places that I preferred high school! Also, the interviewers had nothing about the applicants in front of them except a sheet of paper with names of who was scheduled to visit. So, basically, I sat down and handed them a resume, all of which they hadn't ever seen, and they knew nothing about me. The woman also made it sound as though I was interviewing for a regular education position and not special education. I'm really hoping this isn't what I run into with every district.

Principals may have little control over district office activities; however, they can influence the applicant's interactions with the school. Care needs to be taken to contact applicants early and provide a welcoming and hospitable environment. For example, they should consider arranging for applicants to do observations and have an opportunity to talk with the school staff, offer applicants tours of the school's community, and follow up after the interview.

Special education teachers may receive numerous job offers. They look for administrators who will be supportive of their efforts and schools that have strong collaborative environments. Kellie Wheeling, a new teacher with a master's degree in special education, states what she is looking for in her first position:

> I hope to find a job in an inviting environment, with motivated colleagues, challenging opportunities, and plentiful resources. I would like to come to a job every day that welcomed not only me, but parents and students as well. Motivated, respectful, and knowledgeable colleagues that share my love for students would be great assets in a job. Having materials as well as support from administration would make for an almost perfect job.

Assemble the Interview Team and Develop Questions

An interview team of three to five members should be formed to plan and conduct teacher interviews. Larger teams may be intimidating. The team should include a special education teacher, a general educator with whom the special education teacher will be working, and others as deemed important by the principal.

Best practice suggests that the same team should:

- Review any local policies about hiring;
- Discuss the importance of avoiding all questions related to age, disabilities, marital status, spouses, or children;
- Review the job description and finalize interview questions;
- Determine guidelines for conducting interviews (e.g., who will ask which questions, use of probes and follow-up questions); and
- Determine how the hiring decision will be made (e.g., individual or group decision).

The team should use the same questions across applicants to facilitate comparison. Figure 3.4 provides an interview protocol that should be helpful in interviewing special education teachers. This guide is designed to help administrators assess special educators' knowledge in a range of areas. It provides examples of open-ended questions in each category as well as things to look for in the applicant's responses.

Figure 3.4   Interview Guide for Special Education Teachers

Areas to assess:	Examples of questions:	Things to look for:
Experience and preparation for position	• Please describe your preparation for this position.	• Formal preparation experiences • Supervised field experiences • Other experience with students with disabilities
State Requirements • Certification • Required tests • Accreditation of college program	*If applicant does not hold certification, ask:* • What are you currently doing to obtain certification; *and/or* • When will you complete certification requirements? • Have you completed your Praxis exam(s) (or other requirement)? • Was your preparation program accredited by NCATE, TEAC, or other agency?	• Certification(s) in area(s) in which they teach *and/or* • Is currently enrolled in program/courses to obtain certification
Teacher dispositions	• How would your students describe you? • Tell us about yourself and what you bring to this position? • What was your biggest challenge in your last job (or internship) and how did you address this challenge?	• Caring, respect, dedication, commitment to students • Interest in continued learning, motivation, thoughtful practices
Teacher roles	• Describe your ideal teaching position. • What do you view as the role of the special educator? • What concerns do you have about filling this role?	• Applicant is a good fit in terms of experience, preparation, and view of their roles
View of special education	• What are characteristics of effective programs for students with disabilities?	• Considers where student is in general curriculum and involves collaboration with others • Begins at a level that is appropriate for the student • Is individually planned and based on students' needs • Involves adapted teaching procedures and materials • Includes ongoing assessment of student performance

(Continued)

Figure 3.4 (Continued)

Areas to assess:	Examples of questions:	Things to look for:
Understanding students with disabilities	• Describe the needs of a student with disabilities that you have worked with over a period of time.	• Shows specific understanding of student needs, such as language and communication academic, behavioral, and social needs
Understanding diversity and working with families	• Describe considerations that you have made in addressing the needs of students (and families) from diverse backgrounds.	• Shows an understanding of how individuals and families may differ (e.g., values, perspectives, way of behaving) • Discusses suggestions for adapting instruction for students from diverse backgrounds
Assessment and monitoring of learning	• Describe specific strategies you have used to assess student learning.	• Knowledge about ongoing assessment • Use of frequent assessment to inform how well instruction is working and when changes might be needed
Collaboration and coteaching	• Tell me about your experiences collaborating with general educators. • Please give me an example of a 1) a situation that worked well, and 2) any challenges that you encountered. • What are various ways that you might collaborate and/or co-teach with general educators?	• Flexibility • Knowledge about collaboration • Specific ideas for working with general educators
Instructional strategies	• What types of teaching strategies have you used in your teaching? • How do you decide which teaching strategies to use?	• Is familiar with a range of teaching strategies • Selects teaching procedures based on research support
Individualized Education Programs (IEP)/ Transition planning	• What components are included in an IEP? • Describe how you would facilitate an IEP meeting. • How would you incorporate transition planning in the IEP?	• Awareness of IEP requirements • Importance of being prepared • Evidence that they value parent input • Awareness of transition plans for students age 14 and above

Figure 3.4 (Continued)

Areas to assess:	Examples of questions:	Things to look for:
Student behavior	• How would you approach working with a student who regularly disrupted a class and refused to cooperate?	• Importance of assessing environmental factors • Systematic approach • Importance of relationships
Paraprofessionals	• Describe how you would establish a positive working relationship with paraprofessionals.	• Importance of communication • Specific ideas for working with paraprofessionals
Assistive technology	• Describe any experiences or training that you have had with using assistive technology.	• Is aware of and understands how assistive technology can be used
Interviewee's questions	• We have spent a lot of time asking you questions; what questions do you have?	

SOURCE: Stronge & Hindman (2003) provide an interview guide for general educators. A modified version of their format was used to develop this interview guide for special education teachers.

Schedule the Interview and Establish the Applicant's Itinerary

Contact the applicant and set up your initial interview and consider activities beyond the typical interview. Consider:

- Encouraging the applicant to bring examples of materials such as lesson plans, a taped lesson, or other relevant materials;
- Inviting other special and general educators, the school psychologist, and paraprofessionals to meet the applicant;
- Scheduling an appointment for the applicant to visit the district special education office and provide a tour of the community; and
- Asking the applicant to teach a lesson (if school is in session).

Confirm the Interview

Send a letter to the applicant confirming the date, time, and place for the interview, as well as any additional scheduled activities. After the interview, let applicants know when they can expect a decision and be sure to follow through within the time frame you specify.

Develop Interview Guidelines

The decision to hire a teacher depends largely upon what happens during the interview. Interviewers need to understand not only the knowledge, skills, and dispositions the special education teacher brings to the job, they also need to understand what the applicant wants in a position. Teachers who have qualifications and experiences that are compatible with their assigned job have a better chance of making a positive adjustment to teaching and staying longer. In addition, well-conducted interviews help administrators not only make decisions about who to hire, but allow the assessment of areas in which the new teacher may need assistance. Specifically, the interview team should:

- Introduce the applicant to each member of the interview team,
- Identify and briefly describe the position for which the applicant is interviewing,
- Use open-ended questions (avoid those that can be answered with yes or no),
- listen as much as possible,
- Give the applicant opportunities to ask questions about the position, and
- Tell the applicant you will get back to them soon, and then followup.

The interview process is the beginning of orientation for new teachers, and administrators need to portray the position accurately. Teresa, a new graduate from our special education teacher preparation program, asked her future employer about specific aspects of the job, including caseload size, extracurricular expectations, availability of a mentor, and resource support. When Teresa found that the job was not as described, she was not only very disappointed, but she lost trust in her administrators.

Consider Match of Teacher to Position

In decentralized hiring, the principal and/or the interview team usually makes the final decision. In some districts, the director of special education may also participate in the decision. When you are fortunate enough to have more than one applicant who meets the criteria for the position, take time to consider which candidate is best prepared for the position.

Caseload Match

Consider how well prepared the teacher is to work with the range of students included on the caseload. Special educators are working with increasingly diverse caseloads, and many teachers have minimal experience with students with specific types of disabilities. In her first year of teaching, our former student Louise struggled as a consulting teacher because she had minimum preparation to work with many of the students on her class roll. Louise suggested that, "I wasn't prepared to work with kids with more severe disabilities. I am spending a lot of time figuring out where to begin with these kids."

School Level Match

Another dimension of match is school level. Special education certification usually allows teachers to work in elementary or secondary settings, yet applicants may not have experience in both areas. For example, Joe, a recent special education graduate, completed his field experiences and his internship in an elementary classroom. He had minimal experience with older students, or with the curriculum demands at the secondary level. Applicants may also have strong preferences about the age range of the children that they teach.

Program Model Match

Another important dimension of match is the range of models for serving students with disabilities. Some students are served in resource or full-time classrooms, while others spend all or most of their time in general education settings. Often teachers who are looking for positions have a preference for working in a particular type of setting.

Applicant Preferences

There are other dimensions of match that should also be considered, including the concerns and interests that the applicant shares during the interview. For example, one spring we interviewed an impressive young woman for a special education position in an urban district. After the interview, she expressed a number of reservations about working in an urban school. Yet interview team members thought she was so outstanding that we worked hard to "sell" her on the position. She signed the contract we offered, but backed out two weeks before school began. We not only had to scramble at the last minute to find a suitable teacher, we also lost the opportunity to hire other qualified applicants who wanted to work in an urban setting. We learned a hard lesson about listening carefully to what prospective teachers say about their preferences.

Teachers Without Adequate Preparation

When hiring someone without full qualifications, look carefully at their credentials. Some of the applicants may actually be well-qualified, while others do not have even basic qualifications. For example, a promising applicant, Evan, has the background and experience for a special education position, but he is waiting to receive certification from the state. Another applicant, Elsa, is also a strong applicant since she has five years of teaching experience and is only a course away from earning the requirements for certification. In this instance, since the qualifications of the two applicants are comparable, interview data and recommendations are needed to fully assess candidates' background, experiences, and expertise.

In summary, taking time to explore specific aspects of an applicant's training, experiences, and preferences will help administrators make informed decisions about whether an applicant is a good fit for a particular position. When the match is not ideal, consider providing the new hire with more intensive supports during the first year.

Job Offers and Compensation

The entire compensation package may make a difference in not only whether or not the applicant accepts the position, but may also contribute to whether or not they stay. Consider involving businesses, community leaders, and parents in the development of strategies to recruit and keep good special educators. Some community members recommend providing increased pay or bonuses for teachers working in special education (Mandlawitz, 2003).

Make salaries as competitive as possible. Special educators who earn more are more likely to stay than those with lower salaries (Boe et al., 1997). Offering a competitive salary is also important to recruitment, since special educators are likely to receive offers from more than one district. Some districts offer differential salaries in high need areas to attract teachers to particular schools and positions. Unfortunately, districts who cannot offer competitive salaries are at a serious disadvantage when it comes to both hiring and retaining teachers. Additional incentives that can be added to the offer are discussed in an earlier section of this chapter.

TIPS FOR LEADERS

Streamline Recruitment and Hiring Processes

Identify each aspect of recruitment and hiring, from recruiting teachers to making offers. Involve school staff in the process as soon as it is feasible. Be organized and systematic since teachers may not pursue positions in districts that are slow to respond to applications or have disorganized hiring processes.

Establish Relationships
With Teacher Preparation Programs

Your contacts with universities may help you recruit teachers. Get to know faculty in the special education programs. Visit university classes, distribute promotional materials, and let faculty know you are interested in supervising interns.

Provide Incentives for Switchers

Recruit general education teachers who are particularly effective in working with students with disabilities into special education. Providing incentives, such as paying for coursework, giving them a step higher on the salary scale, or staying in the same school, may persuade these teachers to switch to special education teaching.

CHAPTER SUMMARY

- Thoughtful recruiting and hiring practices will not only help increase the odds of finding highly qualified special education teachers, but keeping them as well.
- Given the difficulty of finding qualified special educators, leaders need to make the most of the recruitment and hiring process.
- The interview process needs to allow the applicant to demonstrate their knowledge and skills, and allow for extended interactions with the school community.
- Teachers who are in positions which match their qualifications, training, experience, and preferences are more likely to stay than those who are assigned positions that do not match.

- Be ready to offer the best possible salary and incentives that you can.
- What is learned about the applicant during the interview process provides important information that can be used to plan responsive induction programs.

SELECTED READINGS

Enlarging the pool: How higher education partnerships are recruiting and supporting future special educators from underrepresented groups. (2003). Retrieved October 10, 2003 from http://www.special-ed-careers.org/pdf/enlargingth epool.pdf

Geiger, W. L., Crutchfield, M. D., & Mainzer, R. (2003). *The status of licensure of special education teachers in the 21st century.* Retrieved October 20, 2003 from http://www.coe.ufl.edu/copsse/pubfiles/RS-7.pdf

Levin, J., & Quinn, M. (2003). *Missed opportunities: How we keep high-quality teachers out of urban classrooms.* The New Teacher Project. Retrieved October 14, 2003 from http://www.tntp.org/report.html.

Mainzer, R., & Horvath, M. (2001). *Issues in preparing and licensing special educators.* Reston, VA: Council for Exceptional Children.

Rosenberg, M. S., & Sindelar, P. T. (2001). *the proliferation of alternative routes to certification in special education: A critical review of the literature.* Arlington, VA: The National Clearinghouse for the Professions in Special Education.

Tyler, N., Yzquierdo, Z., Lopez-Reyna, N., & Flippin, S. S. (2004). Cultural and linguistic diversity and the special education workforce: A critical overview. *The Journal of Special Education, 38*(1), 22–38.

WEB SITES

AACTE Education Policy Clearinghouse

http://www.edpolicy.org/regional/south/spc.htm

This site is designed to provide users access to education policy and teacher quality information at the national, regional, or state levels.

American Board for Certification of Teacher Excellence

http://www.abcte.org/

This organization provides a Passport to Teaching Certification and is developing a Master Teacher Certification. The intent is to reduce barriers to teaching and to help schools meet the requirements of NCLB. Current certifications include English, mathematics, and elementary education, although the board is planning to expand in other areas such as special education. The Passport is currently accepted in Idaho and Pennsylvania.

Council for Exceptional Children (CEC)

http://www.ncate.org/(http://www.cec.sped.org/ps/

The CEC Web site provides information on the National Council for Accreditation of Teacher Education (NCATE) standards for special education and provides information for employers and job seekers.

Interstate New Teacher Assessment and Support Consortium (INTASC)

http://www.ccsso.org

INTASC provides a forum for its member states to develop knowledge of and collaborate in the development of educational policies, teacher preparation, and professional development.

National Clearinghouse for Professions in Special Education (NCPSE)

http://www.special-ed-careers.org/about_us/index.html

This organization provides information regarding special education personnel preparation, recruitment, and retention. It collects, organizes, and disseminates information regarding personnel needs. Please see NCPSE's Web site for a range of reports and useful documents, such as its recruitment toolkit, available at http://www.special-ed-careers.org/research_library/recruitment_kit.html

National Board for Professional Teaching Standards (NBPTS)

http://www.nbpts.org/

NBPTS is a nonprofit organization governed by a board made up of primarily classroom teachers. Other members include school administrators, school board leaders, governors and state legislators, higher education officials, teacher union leaders, and business and community leaders. The NBPTS Web site provides information about its mission, how to earn the National Board Teaching Certificate, scholarships, and numerous other information about educational reform and the teaching profession.

Oregon Special Education Recruitment and Retention Web site

http://www.tr.wou.edu/rrp/

This project is a collaborative effort between the Oregon Department of Education, Office of Special Education, and Teaching Research at Western Oregon to recruit and retain qualified special education personnel in the state of Oregon. The project Web site contains valuable information about recruitment and retention in special education, and information for employers and job seekers in special education.

Recruiting New Teachers (RNT)

http://www.rnt.org/channels/clearinghouse/

RNT is a nonprofit organization based with the primary mission of raising esteem for teaching, expanding the pool of qualified teachers, and improving the nation's teacher recruitment, development, and diversity policies and practices. The Web site provides a job bank and numerous other information critical to teacher recruitment and retention.

Supporting New Special Educators Through Responsive Induction

4

Although policymakers can mandate and fund recruitment and induction programs, only school leaders can foster the full range of supports that teachers need.

(Johnson & Birkeland, 2003b, p. 24)

S pecial educators are not only difficult to find—they are also hard to keep. Estimates suggest that close to half of all new special education teachers leave during the first five hazardous years (Griffin, Winn, Otis-Wilborn, & Kilgore, 2002). Consequently, one of the most important actions that school districts can take to retain special educators is to provide responsive induction programs in the first years of teaching.

Induction programs can reduce the stress of the first year of teaching and help teachers to develop knowledge and teaching skills. Special educators who describe their induction programs as helpful:

- Are more likely to find their jobs manageable,
- Perceive success in providing services to students with Individualized Education Programs (IEPs),
- Indicate that they can help the most difficult students, and
- Are more likely to stay (Billingsley, 2002; Whitaker, 2000a).

SCENARIO: HOW WE EAT OUR YOUNG

Beth Saunders left her first teaching job at the end of her first year. She entered teaching with a master's degree in special education from a strong teacher preparation program. Beth began her position with minimal guidance from the administration or her more experienced colleagues. Although an experienced special education mentor was assigned to help Beth, her mentor had no training, was rarely available, and provided little support. Beth's main source of support was another beginning special educator in the school. She indicated they were trying to "figure it out together."

Beth had a full caseload of students, with one student with particularly challenging behaviors. Although Beth had a strong desire to help this student, she found little support available. Beth's principal expected her to address this student's needs at any point during the day, even though this sometimes left Beth with little time for her other students.

Beth indicated that the general education teachers made critical decisions about her students without her input. She indicated that it was obvious the "general education teachers don't want to deal with my students or me." By the end of the first semester, Beth was emotionally and physically exhausted. She described her first months as "brutal."

Beth also received little orientation about the district or school. She had to figure out the district processes for completing IEPs as well as the student identification process, and wasn't sure she was "doing it right."

The adverse conditions of Beth's work led her to resign after her first teaching year. Her abrupt entry into a difficult teaching situation without adequate support from her colleagues and principal made what is a typically a difficult year even tougher. Over the first year, continual stress, low satisfaction with her job, and a sense of being ineffective led to Beth's withdrawal. Her first year would have likely been very different had Beth worked with an experienced mentor in a supportive school environment.

CHAPTER OVERVIEW

Induction programs are needed regardless of how well teachers are prepared—all new teachers require some form of support and assistance. New special educators who have well-designed work assignments, receive induction support, and are emotionally supported are more satisfied with their work and develop stronger commitments to their students and schools. This chapter addresses:

- Reasons new teachers struggle,
- Induction goals and planning,

✎ Percent white:		86
✎ Percent female:		78
✎ Median age:		27
✎ Percent with a disability:		11
✎ Percent with MA:		21

Figure 4.1   Characteristics of Beginning Special Education Teachers

SOURCE: Billingsley, 2002.

- Key components of induction programs, and
- Mentor programs for special educators.

REASONS NEW TEACHERS STRUGGLE

Beth's experience illustrates some of the problems and frustrations that new teachers experience, especially when they have inadequate support. Beth begins with the same responsibilities of her more experienced peers. However, unlike these colleagues, she must navigate district and school expectations, establish routines, negotiate her various roles, and determine how to apply what she learned in her teacher preparation program. Even experienced teachers who are new to a district face some of the same issues and stressors as those just graduating college. To add to the challenge of the first year, new teachers are often given the most demanding assignments. This section highlights factors that contribute to the transition shock and stress that many new teachers experience.

The First Year Is a Major Life Transition

Many new teachers are making a major life transition. New teachers are not just transitioning into the world of work; they are leaving college and their established support group. These teachers may have financial concerns, experience feelings of isolation and loneliness, and feel overwhelmed by the many changes in their lives.

New Teachers Experience a Steep Learning Curve

New teachers do not have the knowledge and skills of their more experienced peers. Therefore, in their first year they must adapt to their circumstances and learn quickly (Feiman-Nemser, Schwille, Carter, & Yusko, 1999). Although most new teachers have learned relevant theories and strategies, they struggle with how to apply their knowledge. As one new special educator states, "I felt like I had learned most of the stuff in college, but all of it didn't quite stick. It was stuff that I knew I had learned, but I didn't remember or know exactly how to apply it in my particular situation" (Whitaker, 2000b, p. 29). The learning curve is even steeper for the many unqualified first-year special educators. These unqualified teachers are unfamiliar with best practices, and lack even a basic understanding of what they need to know.

New Teachers Often Find the First Year Overwhelming

New teachers do not have established routines and organizational structures in place. The volume and range of work responsibilities can overwhelm beginning teachers who wonder how they can get it all done. Alex, a first-year special educator reported her first year was "crazy," "stressful," and "exhausting." In addition to her usual teaching-related tasks, she agreed to coach basketball, which she considered a "major error."

New Teachers Are Often Idealistic and Have Unrealistic Expectations

New teachers may have a "textbook" idea of what their job should be like and are often unhappy with aspects of the job that do not meet their expectations. A new special education teacher writes "student teaching had not . . . prepared me for the gap between my idealism and the reality of some teaching cultures" (MacDonald, 2001, p. 89).

Teachers may have unrealistic expectations about what they should be able to accomplish and they often overestimate their ability to cope with the demands placed on them. Miriam, a new middle special educator, was assigned to coteach in four different content area classes, including mathematics, language arts, social studies, and science. She asked optimistically, "Why not do it all at once?" However, later in the year she found coteaching to be the most challenging aspect of her job. She had to study the material because of her lack of content knowledge and stated, "Not knowing the material makes for a lousy lesson sometimes."

New Teachers May Experience Crises and Challenges

New teachers inevitably face unexpected challenges, such as a disgruntled parent, a legal hearing, or figuring out complex testing requirements. Patty, a first-year teacher, was required to attend a due process hearing involving one of her students. She found dealing with advocates stressful and testifying in a hearing "terrifying." She wonders why no one told her this was an aspect of teaching.

New Teachers Think They Should Know

Even with all of the challenges new teachers face, they are often reluctant to seek help. New teachers often have questions but believe they should already know how their schools work, what their students need, and how to teach (Johnson & Kardos, 2002). One special educator stated, "It's hard the first time you go and ask. . . . It kind of makes you feel dumb. . . . I waited a long time before I went and asked because I thought, 'they are going to think I can't handle this'" (Whitaker, 2000b, p. 32). New teachers may be especially reluctant to seek help from administrators, because they are responsible for preparing teacher evaluations.

Many New Teachers Receive Little or Inadequate Support

Many new teachers do not have opportunities to participate in carefully designed induction programs. Despite the shortage of special education teachers and the need to retain them, recent evidence suggests that many new teachers do not receive adequate support (Whitaker, 2003). For example, a nationwide study found that 60% of new special educators had formal mentoring programs available to them. Unfortunately, about one-third of those who received mentoring did not find it especially helpful (Billingsley, Carlson, & Klein, 2004). Some of these special educators likely participated in programs designed for general educators and did not receive assistance tailored to their specific needs.

INDUCTION GOALS AND PLANNING

Well-designed induction programs do more than focus on survival needs—they provide new special educators with professional development opportunities, pedagogical guidance, and ongoing support in critical areas during the first years of teaching. Three important areas of induction planning are addressed in this section:

- Determining the goals of teacher induction,
- Understanding special educators' needs and concerns, and
- Clarifying the roles of both school and district leaders in the induction process.

Determine the Goals of the Induction Program

A well-designed induction program must consider its goals and determine how these goals will be accomplished. Examples of induction goals include:

- Improve student achievement through better teacher performance,
- Promote the well-being of teachers and reduce the isolation and stress that many beginning teachers experience,
- Transmit the culture of the school and school system to new teachers, and
- Increase retention (Arrends & Rigazio-DiGilio, 2000; Griffin et al., 2002).

The district may have other stated goals, such as addressing student diversity, increasing collaboration among general or special education teachers, or meeting state mandates. Encouraging broad input into the goals and design of the induction program should help foster involvement from participants.

Induction programs need to be evaluated. Evaluation should extend beyond measures of participant satisfaction and attempt to measure how well the program helped achieve the goals of the program.

Understand Special Educators' Concerns and Needs

New special educators' concerns can be grouped into four major areas: teaching concerns, organization and management concerns, collaborative concerns, and support concerns (see Figure 4.2). Taking time to learn about the concerns and needs of new special educators allows leaders to be strategic by considering these needs in induction planning. New special educators have many questions such as:

- How can I find reading materials that are both appropriate and interesting to my students?
- What is the IEP process in the district?
- How are students' behavioral issues handled in the school?
- Who will evaluate me?

New Teachers' Needs Vary

Although many special educators experience similar concerns, each special educator is unique, with differing academic abilities, training, beliefs, expectations, and personality attributes (Rosenberg, Griffin,

Pedagogical Concerns

- Assessing student performance and evaluating their progress
- Addressing students' individual needs
- Developing lesson plans
- Developing effective teaching methods
- Understanding the curriculum
- Finding appropriate materials and resources
- Assisting students with complex needs
- Helping students with individual needs versus demands of general curriculum

Organization and Management Issues

- Understanding school and district expectations
- Managing paperwork and noninstructional duties
- Challenges in writing IEPs and fulfilling legal requirements
- Lack of clarity about their roles
- Conflicting demands
- Managing time and stress
- Problems with scheduling
- Large caseloads of students

Collaborative Concerns

- Lack of time to collaborate with general educators
- Challenges in working collaboratively with general educators
- General educators' reluctance to collaborate
- Problems working with paraprofessionals
- Working with and involving parents

Support Issues

- Lack of administrative support
- Feelings of isolation
- Lack of needed resources and materials
- Few professional development opportunities
- Lack of mentor support or inadequate time with mentor
- Understanding the teacher evaluation process

Figure 4.2   Concerns of Beginning Special Education Teachers

SOURCE: Adapted from Billingsley & Tomchin, 1992; Billingsley, 2004

Kilgore, & Carpenter, 1997). The context in which each teacher works and the match between the teachers' background and assignment influence support needs. For example, Lisa was an exceptionally strong new teacher who felt ready for her first teaching position. She had completed a yearlong internship in the school where she was hired, she already knew the teachers, and she had worked as part of the coteaching program. Although Lisa worked with her mentor throughout her first year, she had different needs than her colleague, Rose. Rose was hired at the last minute, had minimal preparation, and lacked knowledge and experience about many aspects of the job. Although Lisa needed support from her mentor,

Rose required more intensive levels of support. Rose met daily with her mentor during the first months of school, enrolled in an online course on teaching methods, and spent time each week observing other teachers.

First-Year Special Educators' Perspectives

On the First Year

"My first year was much tougher than I expected. I had no curriculum, no support, no experienced special education teacher in the building, and no real experience at the district level. . . . I would arrive before the sun came up and leave after dark. By November I called my mom one night just bawling on the phone to tell her I wanted to work at Belks or Winn-Dixie—I didn't care. I was not going back to teach!" (Jessica, from Whitaker, 2000b, p. 28).

On Support

"I have a very good relationship with my principal. He has an open door policy. You can tell him exactly what you think. He's very interested in what's going on. I've gone to him with specific problems and he has been very supportive. He comes to the classroom and visits my students. . . . He may not always give you what you want but he's great" (Mary, from Kilgore, Griffin, Otis-Wilborn, & Winn, 2003, p. 43).

"Special ed teachers feel more isolated. . . . The most important thing we need help with is encouragement and support" (Whitaker, 2000b, p. 30).

On Student Behavior

"[These few students] were so loud that I couldn't get anything else done. They were [noisy] over my voice and the other students [who] were trying to wait patiently are now getting bored and wanting to move on. . . . And that's definitely affecting the other students' learning. It's a terrible feeling" (Kilgore et al., 2003, pp. 40-41).

On Curriculum and Availability of Resources

"I have three preps [science, social studies, and language arts]. The books never came in and the ESE teachers didn't get our books. What we have—the workbooks—are worthless. . . . I am figuring out curriculum without a clue. Creating something on my own is too hard. I've done thousands and thousands of Xeroxes" (Kilgore et al., 2003).

On Collaborating With General Educators

"Some of them take the attitude if they cannot hack it then they should not be in here [the regular classroom]. And those teachers . . . they are not going to change" (Billingsley & Tomchin, 1992, p. 108).

On Paperwork and Procedures

"Nobody helped me fill out the paperwork. I had to figure that out on my own and then send it across the street and have the director send it back and say, 'you didn't do this' or 'you didn't do that.' It was all of the procedural things. . . . That stuff was very hard for me" (Whitaker, 2000b).

Assess New Teachers' Needs

Understanding the unique needs of each special educator begins during the hiring process, as the interview team reviews the applicant's background, listens to the teacher's responses to interview questions, and observes a lesson. Mark, a newly hired high school special education teacher, showed little knowledge of the transition needs of students with disabilities during his interview. Susan, Mark's mentor, was asked to share information with Mark about the transition needs of students and their families, the district's program, and special educators' roles in the transition process. Susan also invited Mark to assist her as she worked with a student and his family on a transition program.

Special educators' needs will change throughout the first year. Listening to teachers, observing them, and learning about their needs through discussions, observations, and informal surveys can help administrators and mentors determine the types of support that may be helpful. Specific assessments can also be used to identify areas in which the special educator needs assistance, and special educators should be encouraged to request assistance in areas of need.

Specify School and District Leaders' Roles in Inducting Special Educators

School and district leaders need to coordinate their efforts to ensure that a range of induction supports are available to new special educators.

Although induction programs are often organized at the district or state level, principals and mentors are in the best position to support special education teachers on a daily basis.

Facilitate the Vision, Structures, and Support for Induction

District leaders facilitate induction by working for a coherent structure, securing financial and other forms of support, and allocating resources. For example, administrative considerations include:

- Providing a strong conceptualization of the induction program,
- Gathering broad input into the goals for the induction program,
- Determining length of induction program (preferably beyond one year),
- Determining who is eligible to participate (new teachers and experienced teachers who are new to the district), and
- Developing policies about how mentors will be selected, trained, rewarded, and recognized.

District leaders should consider districtwide supports for new special educators, such as scheduling new teacher support groups, planning specific professional development activities, and scheduling observations for special educators who do not have experienced mentors in their schools. District administrators are in the best position to assess new special educators' needs across the district.

District leaders may also want to pursue the development of university-school induction partnerships for teacher induction and mentoring. These partnerships allow for shared expertise and resources that benefit both agencies (see the following Textbox for an interview with Lynn Boyer about the development of such linkages).

Developing University-School Collaborations for Special Education Teacher Induction

*Dr. K. Lynn Boyer**

1. *In what ways are university-school collaborations helpful to the development of induction programs for special educators?*
An important message is established when induction programs are developed through a university-school collaboration or partnership. The university and the local school district demonstrate

through this collaboration the recognition that induction into the profession begins during preparation and continues through the early years in the profession, and that teacher education is the responsibility of both the university and the local school district. Induction begins not during orientation in August, but throughout the preparation period and the early years in the classroom.

University-school collaboration facilitates the transition between learning to teach and teaching confidently and effectively. It reflects a shared commitment to induct aspiring and novice teachers into the field, providing the security of instructional support, application of research to practice, insight of practitioners working with specific areas of disabilities, and multiple resources that are close at hand. University-school collaboration can increase both the financial and human resources available for this transition work. The willingness to be creative in the use of these resources is always, however, a fundamental challenge.

2. What is needed to foster the development of these university-school partnerships?

As with any joint venture, success is more likely when the work meets concomitant needs. A project in Colorado provides a good example of this. The university wanted a means by which to build a cadre of special educators who were deeply sensitive to the needs of students in urban schools, and a nearby urban school district wanted special educators who would be prepared to help them create a successful inclusion initiative in its schools. A collaborative project was born that supported over 100 special educators in five years and that, in the process, resulted in the redesign of the university's preparation program.

Those involved in the collaboration must have unflagging support from both agencies, committed leadership, and a deeply shared vision for teacher development. Participants in programs that have longevity and positive outcome data demonstrate through their actions uncommon persistence, relentless communication, and sustained focus. Creative funding is, again, a hallmark of these programs. That says to me that there is also a strong inclination to be flexible!

A university-school partnership must address the variety of skills, abilities, and preparation that aspiring or novice special educators are bringing to classrooms now. A partnership-based induction program now is frequently meeting the needs of persons choosing to become a special educator after acquiring a bachelor's degree in a noneducation field, teaching in another discipline, or returning to the field with a lapsed license after a hiatus. This gets back to my earlier point that the needs of each agency have to be clear at the outset, and the commitment to a common goal must be well established.

3. What are some of the challenges that universities and schools face in the development of these partnerships?

These partnerships or collaborative programs are complex because, by their nature, many people are involved. Both general education and special education faculty and staff have roles. The school district's human resources department must be at the table because of the licensure issues, potential for creation of mentor positions, and salary considerations of the new teachers or interns participating in the program. As the program moves to individual schools, administrators and teachers who will have responsibilities must be represented. Maintaining the momentum of the partnership, keeping the focus as a driving force, and coordinating the multiple parties is time intensive and physically demanding.

A significant challenge is agreeing on the characteristics or components of the induction program. A growing body of research identifies aspects of induction programs that teachers evaluate as helpful or beneficial and that partnerships view as contributing to retention of teachers. There is scant work, however, on the components of induction programs that are of particular importance and value to special educators. There is virtually no research as yet on the impact on student achievement from teachers who have been in specifically designed induction programs. A partnership does not want to invest financial or human resources in induction programs that will not improve the achievement of students or the retention of its teachers.

A challenge that arises after a university-school collaboration is established is the disinclination of one or the other to expend the time necessary to sustain it. When this happens, the needs of the participating teachers have to be paramount as a decision is made to dissolve the partnership.

4. What advice do you have for university and school administrators in the development of induction partnerships?

When possible, take advantage of already established partnerships to identify contacts, ascertain interest, investigate resources, and probe for challenges that have been overcome in the past.

Maximize resources by coming to the partnership with a willingness to consider resources in a creative way. A university in Florida worked in partnership with a local school district to transfer university funds to pay adjuncts to the school district to hire mentor teachers. The mentor teachers could provide more on-site daily supervision than the adjuncts had been able to do, and the needs of the new teachers were better met.

Establish a partnership infrastructure that distributes responsibilities, thereby heightening commitment and infusing the processes into multiple offices. Although the operation of the partnership should be vested in recognized leaders from both agencies, broadly dispersed responsibilities may reduce the impact when key partnership personnel inevitably move on to other positions.

*Lynn Boyer, PhD, is executive director, Office of Special Education, West Virginia Department of Education

Principals and Mentors Need to Create a Climate of Support

Principals who lack knowledge of special education may feel uncomfortable assisting and assessing special education teachers and, therefore, take a hands-off approach. However, clarifying the expectations for the special education program, visiting special education classrooms, and discussing the needs of students with disabilities will help new special educators feel that they are a part of the school.

Emphasize Emotional Support

Special educators are less likely than other new teachers to indicate that they feel a sense of belonging in their schools (Billingsley et al., 2004). Because special educators often feel isolated, an essential part of induction includes emotional support (Gold, 1996; Whitaker, 2003). Emotional support is one of the most valued types of support and includes maintaining open communication, taking an interest in the teachers' work, considering their ideas, and showing appreciation for their efforts (Littrell, Billingsley, & Cross, 1994).

KEY COMPONENTS OF INDUCTION PROGRAMS

Mentoring is the most common form of support. However, other activities are needed to support new special educators. These include:

- Orientation programs,
- School support teams,
- Peer support meetings,
- Professional development opportunities, and
- Support from a mentor teacher.

These forms of support provide teachers with essential information about their roles as well as helping them to problem solve and develop new skills. A word of caution—too many induction activities can be overwhelming as well as counterproductive. Be sure to explicitly differentiate between induction activities that are voluntary and those that are required.

"Christine's support through her first year of teaching came from multiple levels. Her induction program provided continued professional development and the physical presence of a mentor who knew exactly what she was experiencing in a classroom for students with autism. The mentor provided tangible administrative help with IEPs and instructional support in adapting curricula and designing unique lessons to meet individual student needs. Christine's principal and assistant principal were supportive with their time, school resources, opportunities to be part of decisions, and insight into the struggles she was facing each day. Her school district provided support with technology, program expertise, and administrative resources. Christine came to her first year of teaching exceptionally well prepared, yet acknowledges that she needed all the supports she got to convert her challenges into successes" (Boyer & Lee, 2001, p. 83).

New Teacher Orientation

Special and general educators benefit from learning as much about their districts, school(s), and communities as possible. Orientation can include information that helps teachers better understand their work environments (e.g., tours of the community, written materials, meetings, and informal discussions).

Special Education District Orientation Meeting

New special educators report that their area of greatest need is learning the mechanics of the job, which includes understanding district and school policies (Whitaker, 2003). District administrators should hold an orientation meeting for all special education teachers in the district. Figure 4.3 (from the Oregon Recruitment/Retention Project) outlines information that should be shared with special educators, including the roles of support staff, the philosophy of the special education program, and procedures for ordering instructional materials. Question and answer sessions should be part of orientation so that new teachers are given an opportunity to have their concerns addressed. A district-level orientation should be held prior to the start of school. If an orientation is not provided, the principal or mentor should review the items outlined in Figure 4.3.

Resources that will help the special educator, such as a district manual, guides for new special educators, and applicable Web sites should be shared at the orientation meeting. Schedule an informal social after the meeting to encourage new teachers to meet their mentors and other new teachers.

School Orientation

The principal or mentor needs to review important policies, such as the school's mission statement, attendance and discipline policies, and procedures for handling emergencies (see Figure 4.3). General policies should be discussed with all new teachers in the school; however, it is important that the special education teacher be familiar with special education functions and policies.

A critical component of the district and school orientation is to explain the roles of the principal and district administrators in the leadership of special education programs. Special educators need to know who to contact for legal advice, who usually attends IEP meetings, and how to order necessary materials. Further, new special educators need information about the roles that district leaders and principals play in the evaluation of their performance.

Mentoring

Mentoring is often included in new teacher induction programs. Even with the growing interest in mentor programs, many special educators do not have access to mentor programs and about one-third of those who do, indicate that it is of limited value (Billingsley et al., 2004). Unfortunately, mentoring programs are sometimes initiated without careful planning. Special education mentors may spend little time with new special educators, have few opportunities for observations (Meyer, 2004), and spend little time in their classrooms. The next section of this chapter discusses the development of special education mentor programs.

Providing ongoing support for early career educators during the first three years of teaching is of critical importance toward their retention. The level of administrative and peer support is a significant factor in retaining early career special educators. Research shows that beginning educators need the following:

- System information related to special education
- Emotional support
- System information related to the school, materials, curriculum, and instruction

Orientation to Special Education

Beginning special educators should receive an orientation developed and conducted by special education administrators that provides the following information:

- Special education district/agency mission and philosophy
- Roles and responsibilities of key personnel
- District/agency expectations (educator roles and responsibilities)
- Characteristics (culture) of special education department
- Introduction of district support staff
- Special education support staff availability and how to access
- Paperwork requirements, procedures, and timelines (sample forms, i.e., IEP form)
- Assessment and referral process for children with suspected disabilities
- Student records policies (confidentiality, storage, etc.)
- Available materials and other resources (audiovisual equipment, instructional materials, resource centers, etc.)
- Procedures for ordering supplies, equipment, instructional materials
- Staff list

The special education orientation meeting should include the beginning special educator and special education administrators from the school district and should be held prior to the beginning of the school year.

Orientation to School and District

Early educators, along with their peers in regular education, should participate in orientation covering general district information. This orientation will serve to assist the early educator to become familiar with the building's policies and procedures, the physical facility, administrators, and other key building staff. This orientation should cover the following:

- Overview of school, including mission and philosophy
- Characteristics (culture) of school
- Roles and responsibilities of key school personnel
- Supervisory role and responsibilities of the building administrator/principal in relation to special education staff
- School discipline procedures along with policies related to the discipline of special education students
- Extracurricular activities/expectations
- Clerical/secretarial staff availability and how to access them
- Process used to refer children with suspected disabilities
- Student records policies (confidentiality, storage, etc.)
- Available materials and other resources (audiovisual equipment, instructional materials, resource centers, etc.)
- Procedures for ordering supplies, equipment, instructional materials
- Staff list

Figure 4.3   Orientation for New Special Educators

SOURCE: From the Oregon Special Education Recruitment and Retention Project http://www.tr.coou.edu/rrp/teachersupport.htm. Used with permission.

School Support Team

New teachers indicate that other teachers are their most valued source of support (Billingsley et al., 2004). In addition to the special education teacher mentor program, two or three additional teachers or staff at the school should be assigned to support the special educator during the first year to make sure that his or her concerns and needs are being addressed.

The support team can assist the new teacher by:

- Helping the teacher feel part of the school community,
- Answering questions when the mentor is unavailable, and
- Providing perspectives different from the mentor.

The support team should be comprised of two or three teachers in addition to the special education mentor. New teachers enjoy the support of those with fewer years of experience as well as more experienced teachers (Hertzog, 2002). It is not unusual for new teachers to seek out other teachers with similar levels of experience. When determining the composition of the support team, consider

- A more experienced teacher, as well as a teacher who has recently been mentored;
- A general education teacher who has experience with collaboration; and
- Support personnel such as guidance counselors or psychologists.

Peer Support Meetings

New teachers often benefit from regular opportunities to solve problems and share experiences with other new special educators in the district; this may also be facilitated by exchanging e-mail addresses.

Professional Development Opportunities

Professional development opportunities are an integral part of the induction program. Ideally, an early emphasis on professional development will foster teachers' commitment to continued growth throughout their careers. New teachers and their experienced colleagues need opportunities to examine assessment, teaching, and collaborative issues in their schools. As Johnson and Kardos (2002) state:

What new teachers want in their induction is experienced colleagues who will take their daily dilemmas seriously, watch them teach and provide feedback, help them develop instructional strategies, model skilled teaching, and share insights about students' work and lives. What new teachers need is sustained, school-based professional development—guided by expert colleagues, responsive to their teaching, and continual through the early years in the classroom. Principals and teacher leaders have the largest roles to play in fostering such experiences (p. 13).

Special education teachers also need professional development opportunities geared to their specific needs. Specific content geared toward new special educators includes behavior management, collaboration, adapting instruction, learning strategies, cooperative learning, social skills, motivation strategies, instruction, and interpersonal communication (Gibb & Welch, 1998). New special educators may need to visit programs outside their schools to see well-developed collaborative teams, observe experienced special educators as they teach, and use specialized instructional resources.

Mentor Programs for Special Educators

Specific considerations for the development of mentor programs in special education are described in this section. Many of these considerations are summarized in *The Mentoring Induction Principles Implementation Checklist* (White & Mason, 2001). This checklist is designed to help leaders assess various aspects of their mentor programs (see Figure 4.5 at end of chapter).

Special Educators Need Special Education Mentors

Beginning special educators need to work with experienced special educators. Ideally, the mentor and new teacher work in the same school, so the new teacher can receive timely help. However, when a qualified mentor is not available or willing to help in the school, special educators should be assigned to a mentor in another school (Whitaker, 2003; White & Mason, 2001). When the special education mentor is in another school, it is critical that the mentor and the teacher schedule regular meetings and communicate via e-mail.

Special Education Mentors Must Be Carefully Selected

Strong mentors have the knowledge, skills, and dispositions needed to form supportive and caring relationships (Rowley, 1999). Determining explicit criteria for mentor selection is critical, and many school systems have interviews designed to select the best possible mentors. Special educators with National Board Certification should be considered as mentors because these mentors are prepared to discuss the "whys" about using teaching strategies and assessing specific outcomes (National Boards Set Standards for Teachers, 2004).

The following criteria (Rowley, 1999; White & Mason, 2001) should be considered when selecting mentors:

- Desires to be a mentor and is committed to participate in all aspects of the mentor program,
- Is a highly qualified teacher and viewed as capable by others,
- Has a minimum of three years of *special education* teaching experience,
- Has experience with the same population of students (e.g., learning disabilities, autism) at a similar school level (e.g., elementary, secondary),
- Demonstrates care and commitment toward students,
- Is interested in his or her own learning,
- Communicates hope and optimism, and
- Has an open, flexible, and supportive personality.

Leaders may not find mentors who meet these criteria in smaller school districts or in low incidence areas (e.g., autism, vision impairments). In these cases it can be helpful to work with other districts and universities to help find out-of-district co-mentors who may assist with specific needs.

Mentors Have Varied Roles

Mentoring supports the teacher through the first years of teaching. Mentors have been described as guides, models, listeners, observers, and sources of practical suggestions. In the Utah State Mentoring special education program, teachers perceive mentors as confidants and consultants who give suggestions, model techniques, coach, and offer moral support. Mentors create an atmosphere of sensitivity and support in their schools and model acceptance of individuals with differences (Gibb & Welch, 1998).

Mentors should observe new teachers often, help them analyze their teaching and assess students' progress toward goals, and find solutions to problems. They help new teachers manage complex schedules, collaborate with general educators, and juggle various school requirements.

Ideally, new teachers will work with their mentors on a daily basis. Schools use a range of options for freeing teachers' time. Some use full-time mentor teachers or part-time retired teachers. Others expect mentors to manage full-time teaching positions as well as their work as mentors.

Mentors Need Preparation for Their Roles

Mentors need knowledge, skills, and dispositions to support and coach new teachers (Rowley, 1999). Mentors often receive training and materials to guide them in their work with new teachers. The following topics are often included in mentor training sessions or courses:

- Roles of the mentor (see Figure 4.4 for a description),
- Stages of teacher development,
- Theories of adult learning,
- Research-based teaching methods,
- Typical problems that new special educators experience,
- Suggestions for establishing trust and assuring confidentiality,
- Relationship-building activities,
- Specific strategies for providing instructional support (e.g., clinical supervision, coaching, using pre- and postobservation conferences),
- Materials and resources to share with new teachers (e.g., school policies, IEP forms, stress-management strategies), and
- School orientation meetings for certain procedures (e.g., completing IEPs, grade reports).

A relationship based on trust and respect is essential for the mentor-mentee relationship to work well. Relationships that are collaborative allow both the mentor and the mentee to benefit from the relationship. When the mentor-mentee relationship is poor, another mentor may need to be assigned.

Attend training sessions on mentoring

Attend district meetings on mentoring

Schedule regular times to meet with mentee

Schedule observations and conferences

Provide information to mentee on all school and special education policies

Assist mentee with IEPs and invite mentee to observe an IEP meeting

Provide formative feedback on performance (not to be used for formal evaluation)

Document meetings and activities scheduled with mentee

Maintain confidentiality

Figure 4.4   Special Education Mentor Role Description

Many guides and books have been developed for mentors, yet little has been developed about special education mentoring. Although the mentoring process will be largely the same for general and special education teachers, the *content* of what is discussed may be very different (e.g., completing diagnostic assessments, IEPs).

Mentor Relationships Should Be Supportive, Not Evaluative

Teacher mentoring should not be evaluative; rather, mentoring should be designed to help new teachers grow and develop in their new roles (Griffin et al., 2002; White & Mason, 2001). The development of trusting relationships is an essential part of mentor support, so early agreements about confidentiality should be established between mentors and mentees.

Mentors Should Be Rewarded for Their Efforts

Some districts provide mentors with additional professional development days or support to attend professional conferences (Rowley, 1999). Others may receive a stipend for their training and additional responsibilities, or receive graduate credit for their work as mentors. Districts that do not compensate mentors tend to discourage teachers from serving in these roles, especially when salary supplements are given to those serving as department chairs, coaches, and advisors (Youngs, 2003).

Tips for Leaders and Mentors

Tips for leaders and mentors are provided in three areas: emotional support, the organizational and managerial aspects of the job, and assistance in critical areas of practice. These forms of support may be distributed across principals, mentors, and teacher support team members.

Provide Emotional Support

New special educators often experience isolation and may not feel a sense of belonging in their schools (Billingsley et al., 2004). Providing emotional support is an important antidote to isolation and can be easily provided.

Create a Welcoming School Environment. At the beginning of the year principals should take specific actions to let new special educators know they are a valued part of the school community. Encouraging other members of the teacher's support team to welcome and include the new teacher is also important. Welcoming a special education teacher takes little effort and can make a big difference in helping the new teacher feel at home.

Let New Teachers Know You Are Available to Help. Let the new special educator know that you (and others) are available to answer questions and assist as needed. Listen to and communicate with the new teacher frequently, especially during the first few months of school. Stopping by at the beginning or the end of the day or after a faculty meeting shows interest in the new teacher's needs and adjustment to the school.

Facilitate Informal Interactions and Socialization. Successful induction programs have a culture of shared responsibility for teacher induction, and experienced teachers willingly help newcomers. Some aspects of new teacher socialization occur informally. Encouraging the school staff to welcome and encourage new teachers by providing opportunities for informal interactions will help the new teacher develop a broader range of relationships.

Listen to Teachers. Carefully consider what teachers say and ask teachers how you can help. In peer support meetings ask new teachers to make a list of areas in which they need help. New teachers may be more comfortable bringing up concerns as they work with others who have similar needs.

Treat the New Teacher as a Professional. New teachers need assistance, but it is important not to be too heavy-handed with help. Let new teachers know that the district and school are committed to supporting them, but allow them to help shape this support. Mentor-mentee relationships can go sour if new teachers are treated without parity and respect.

Recognize New Teachers' Accomplishments. Encouragement is particularly important for new teachers who may not be as confident and worry about how they are judged. Remember to notice what is going well.

Provide Support in Managing the Varied Demands of the First Year

Special education teachers often manage a large volume of paperwork, testing, and coordination of legal requirements in addition to their teaching. Managing these bureaucratic requirements is one of the most stressful areas that new special educators encounter. Leaders can help by reducing the initial workload and ensuring that teachers have necessary information for their work.

Reduce Role Expectations in the First Year. Leaders can reduce role expectations by limiting the teachers' number of preparations (e.g., reduce the number of coteaching subjects), reducing the caseload, or providing the teacher with additional planning time (e.g., extra paid days before school begins, an extra hour to plan and collaborate with mentor). Try to refrain from giving new teachers extracurricular assignments.

Provide Written Resources. District leaders should provide teachers with electronic resources or handbooks outlining district and school procedures (e.g., who to contact for help, how to order materials). Providing guidelines for effective practices in key areas, such as working with paraprofessionals and collaborating with general education teachers, can also help special educators get off to a good start. Several guides are published for new special educators (see the following Textbox).

Selected Guides for New Special Educators

Cohen, M. K., Gale, M., & Meyer, J. M. (1994). *Survival Guide for the First-Year Special Education Teacher,* Revised. Council for Exceptional Children, pp. 1-17 (ISBN 0-86586-256-7) 1-888-232-7733.

Pierangelo, R. (1994). *Survival Kit for the Special Education Teacher.* West Nyack, NY: Center for Applied Research in Education.

Rosenberg, M. S., O'Shea, L., & O'Shea, D. (2001*). Student Teacher to Master Teacher* (3rd Ed.). Upper Saddle River NJ: Prentice-Hall.

Shelton, C. F., & Pollingue, A. B. (2001). *The Exceptional Teacher's Handbook: The First-Year Special Education Teacher's Guide for Success.* Thousand Oaks, CA: Corwin Press.

Provide Assistance With Organization, Time Management, and Stress. Help the new teacher develop a sense of what needs to happen in the first few months of school. For example, provide a list of due dates for IEPs or provide a calendar that has major activities filled in (e.g., meeting time with mentor, faculty meetings). The new teacher guides listed in Textbox 4.4 provide ideas for managing the job, addressing paperwork, and establishing priorities. Reducing stress requires that new teachers not only have positive work environments, but learn to handle the pressures and stresses of teaching (see Chapter 8).

Offer Assistance With Scheduling. Scheduling time with general educators and students is often stressful for new and experienced teachers. Provide special educators with sample schedules, allow them opportunities to have input into the master schedule, or, at the secondary level, let them individually schedule their students.

Provide Assistance in Critical Areas of Knowledge and Practice

The following suggestions address some of the most frequently voiced concerns from new special education teachers. Some of these areas can be introduced during orientation; others areas, such as assisting with IEPs, requires more support.

Support Teachers in Understanding the Implications of Federal and State Laws. The requirements of IDEA and the NCLB are stressful for teachers, parents, and students. Little is known about the implications of the new NCLB law for special education teachers and their families. Some worry that the pressures of the new law and conflicts between the law and IDEA will contribute to even greater teacher attrition. Leaders and mentors can reduce the stress by:

- Helping teachers understand what curriculum standards are used in the state and district,
- Clarifying the local and state testing program,
- Sharing information about the test schedule, and
- Reviewing testing accommodations that can be used with students with disabilities.

Review the General Education Curriculum. Given the new emphasis on inclusion and general education curriculum access, special educators should become familiar with the local curriculum. Sharing curriculum with teachers prior to the beginning of the year provides time for teachers to understand state and local standards and the assessment process.

Provide Assistance With Collaboration. Collaboration with general education teachers is one of the most challenging aspects of special educators' work. New special educators sometimes feel awkward in collaborating with more-experienced teachers, or they may lack experience in addressing some of the challenges that occur in collaborative and coteaching situations. Ella, a first-year special education teacher, was surprised when a general teacher said, "I've got this student I think you should observe." Ella commented, "They have been teaching 15 years and they think I can do something with the students they can't." Leaders can help by:

- Setting the stage for strong collaborative practices in the school,
- Providing guidelines for collaboration during teacher orientation,
- Helping new teachers with assistance in addressing collaboration challenges, and
- Encouraging mentor teachers to include special education teachers in their collaborative work, so their actions can help serve as a model for the new teachers.

Clarify Teacher Roles. The principal and mentor teachers should discuss the special educator's roles and responsibilities in the school. New teachers who know what is expected and how to direct their energy will feel a sense of purpose and are less likely to experience role ambiguity and conflict (see Chapter 7). For example:

- Begin with an existing role description for initiating this discussion (see Chapter 7 for examples),
- Ask new teachers how they see their roles,
- Highlight roles that are critical in the first weeks of school, and
- Be sensitive to new teachers' ideas about their roles and indicate your openness to revisions.

Provide Guidelines for IEP Development. Unfortunately, many beginning special educators have neither attended an IEP meeting nor written IEPs (Whitaker, 2003). A districtwide orientation to this process should clarify requirements. New teachers should also be informed about the role of district and school leaders in the IEP process. Be sure to:

- Provide guidelines for developing IEPs,
- Give teachers copies of model IEPs,
- Make sure teachers have necessary forms,
- Involve the new teacher in an IEP meeting with a mentor teacher, and
- Alert new teachers to timelines for development.

Assist With Student Behavior. New teachers find dealing with student behavior one of the most difficult aspects of their work. New teachers often need assistance in building relationships with students, establishing expectations, and preventing problems. Helping new teachers to problem solve about students' behavioral requirements is a high priority need for new teachers.

Help New Teachers Secure Needed Materials and Resources. One of the most pressing issues a new special educator must address is securing adequate teaching and student resources. Classrooms are sometimes stripped of whatever remained by other teachers before the new teacher arrives. New teachers may not know how to secure materials, or know what materials are available or appropriate. The quantity of materials is less important than the quality of materials. "It is better to have fewer excellent resources and to be able to use them well, than to have extensive resources and become overwhelmed by all the ideas presented" (Maroney, 2000, p. 26). Mentors and leaders can assist by

- Providing the new teacher with an inventory of materials available,
- Surveying the needs of new teachers early in the year, and
- Letting teachers know during orientation how instructional resources can be obtained.

Provide Guidelines for Working With Paraprofessionals. Many new teachers are not prepared to work with paraprofessionals, and some express apprehension about working and supervising these assistants. Although paraprofessionals can be an important source of help for new teachers, conflicts may occur that create additional stress. Leaders can help by sharing job descriptions for paraprofessionals (see Chapter 7) and providing guidelines for working with paraprofessionals.

Assist With Guidelines for Communicating With Parents. Some of the new guides for new special educators provide examples of letters of introduction to parents and guardians, guidelines for communicating with parents, suggestions for planning parent-teacher conferences, and suggestions on how to involve parents in the IEP process (see Textbox 4.4). New teachers particularly need support when they experience problems communicating with parents. Leaders may support the teacher by discussing ways of addressing the specific issue and by participating in meetings with parents.

Explain the Teacher Evaluation Process. New teachers are concerned about how they will be evaluated. These beginners need to understand both formative and summative assessments, the roles that leaders and mentors play in the teacher evaluation system, and how they will receive feedback in their first year. Many suggest that mentors provide only formative assistance and do not have input into the teacher evaluation process (Griffin et al., 2002).

SUMMARY

- Supporting new special education teachers is one of the most important ways for leaders to foster teacher retention and quality.

- Well-designed induction programs have wide-ranging benefits, from helping new teachers get off to a positive start to increasing the achievement in the students under their care.
- Special educators have unique needs and require specialized supports.
- Responsive induction programs improve teacher quality through individualized supports that address the needs of the teacher in the context in which the teacher works.
- Induction activities include school and district orientations, meetings with new teachers, administrative supports, and ongoing mentoring by other qualified special educators.
- Special education teachers need qualified, willing, and experienced special education mentors.

SELECTED READINGS

Billingsley, B. S. (2002). *SPeNSE summary sheet. Beginning special educators: Characteristics qualifications, and experiences.* Retrieved March 15, 2002 from www.spense.org.

Billingsley, B., Carlson, E., & Klein, S. (2004). The working conditions and induction support of early career special educators. *Exceptional Children, 70*(3), 333–347.

Boyer, L., & Gillespie, P. (2000). Keeping the committed: The importance of induction and support programs for new special educators. *Teaching Exceptional Children, 33*(1), 10–15.

Boyer, L., & Lee, C. (2001). Converting challenge to success: Supporting a new teacher of students with autism. *The Journal of Special Education, 35*(2), 75–83.

Griffin, C. C., Winn, J. A., Otis-Wilborn, A., & Kilgore, K. L. (2002). *New teacher induction in special education.* Gainesville, FL: University of Florida, Center on Personnel Studies in Special Education (COPSSE).

Maroney, S. A. (2000). What's good? Suggested resources for beginning special education teachers. *Teaching Exceptional Children, 33*(1), 22–27.

Whitaker, S. D. (2000a). Mentoring beginning special education teachers and the relationship to attrition. *Exceptional Children, 66*(4), 546–566.

WEB SITES

Beginning and Preservice Teachers

http://www.sabine.k12.la.us/vrschool/newteachers.htm

This Web site provides many helpful resources for mentors and helping new teachers get off to a good start.

Beginning Special Educators (IRIS Star Legacy Module)

http://iris.peabody.vanderbilt.edu/beginteach/chalcycle.htm

This online multimedia module helps administrators, principals, and mentors understand the needs of beginning special educators. Numerous interviews, perspectives on new teachers, and strategies for administrators to use in supporting new teachers are provided. This module is appropriate to use as a component of special education mentor training.

Council or Exceptional Children (CEC)

http://www.cec.sped.org/spotlight/udl/mip_g_manual_11pt.pdf

The Council for Exceptional Children's Web site provides "Mentoring and Induction" Guidelines (developed by Marlene White and Christine Mason).

Mentoring Leadership and Resource Network

www.mentoring.net

The Association for Supervision and Curriculum Development free advice network is dedicated to supporting educators with best practices in mentoring and induction.

Oregon Recruitment/Retention Project

http://www.tr.wou.edu/rrp/

This Web site provides a range of materials for administrators interested in supporting beginning special educators, including advice for district and school administrators, as well as guidelines for developing a mentor program.

Essential Features of the Mentoring Program		
Feature:	Component Included in Program:	Notes:
Collaborative Development: Clear Mentoring Program objectives were developed collaboratively.		
Awareness: Information on roles, expectations, policies, provisions, and desired outcomes is shared and understood by all stakeholders.		
Adequate Resources: Human and fiscal resources have been anticipated and budgeted.		
Full Participation: All first-year special educators are expected to participate.		
Coordination Among Programs: Mentoring of special educators is coordinated with other mentoring programs but addresses special education concerns.		
Process-Based: Relationship between mentor and new special educator is for support and guidance. The mentor has no formal evaluation responsibilities.		

Figure 4.5   The Mentoring Induction Checklist

Figure 4.5 (Continued)

Essential Features of the Mentoring Program

Feature:	Component Included in Program:	Notes:
Responsibility: District level person is given specific responsibilities to coordinate and oversee mentoring program.		
Compensation: Mentors receive compensation based on choices.		
Evaluation: Feedback obtained from mentoring team used to make recommended changes.		

Mentor Selection: Qualities and Characteristics of Mentor Teachers

The Mentor:
- must be a special education teacher
- preferably in:
  - ✓ same school
  - ✓ teaching same population
  - ✓ at same grade level
- should be a volunteer
- should have 3–5 years special education experience in current district
- is viewed as a master teacher by the school administrator

ORIENTATION AND TRAINING

BEGINNING SPECIAL EDUCATION TEACHERS

Beginning special educators hired prior to school openings participate with mentors in inservice and planning before school opens. Beginning special educators hired after school openings are paired with mentors and provided orientation to the program as soon as possible.

Beginning special educators have the opportunity to meet regularly with other new teachers to share materials, strategies, successes, and concerns.

Professional development for beginning special educators includes:

- behavior management techniques
- IEP development and implementation
- curriculum and lesson planning
- special education laws and administrative responsibilities
- assessment procedures
- school and district policies and procedures
- organization and time management techniques
- collaboration with professional colleagues, including paraeducators, and parents.

Figure 4.5 (Continued)

Mentor Teacher training			
Each mentor works with only one beginning special educator per year.			
Mentor teachers have opportunity to meet regularly with other mentors to share materials, strategies, successes, and concerns.			
Mentor teacher training includes: • role and expectations of the mentor • needs of beginning special educators • the role and responsibilities of beginning special educators in the mentoring process • effective communication skill development incorporating adult learning principles • consultation strategies, including constructive feedback and social support • time management and organizational strategies • classroom observation skills • updates on IEP development and program implementation • updates on special education laws and administrative requirements • advising and coaching skills • behavior management strategies across grade levels and disabilities • collaboration and problem-solving skills • instructional strategies, including accommodations and modifications for content			

92

ROLES AND RESPONSIBILITIES OF MENTORING TEAM		
BEGINNING SPECIAL EDUCATOR	<ul><li>attends all training sessions</li><li>requests assistance proactively</li><li>schedules and attends sessions with mentor teacher</li><li>remains open and responsive to feedback/suggestions</li><li>observes other teachers</li><li>conducts self-assessment and uses reflective skills</li><li>participates in evaluation of program</li></ul>	
MENTOR TEACHER	<ul><li>attends all training sessions</li><li>provides support and guidance</li><li>acclimates beginning special educator to school and community culture</li><li>observes beginning teacher regularly</li><li>provides postobservation feedback in timely manner</li><li>models appropriate classroom and professional behaviors</li><li>maintains professional and confidential relationship</li><li>participates in evaluation of program</li></ul>	

Figure 4.5 (Continued)

Figure 4.5 (Continued)

MENTOR PROGRAM COORDINATOR		

• manages the mentoring program
• ensures building administrators are informed and supportive
• develops district recommended procedures for mentoring
• guides development and adoption of resource materials and schedules
   inservice training for beginning special educators and mentors
• arranges and conducts regular meetings with new teachers and mentors
• ensures implementation, evaluation, and improvement
   of mentoring program
• helps provide more intensive support for individual special
   education and mentor teachers as needed		

BUILDING ADMINISTRATOR		
• attends orientation session on mentoring implementation • provides release time for beginning special educators and mentors to observe and conference with each other • observes and facilitates mentoring relationship • nominates only master teachers as mentors • offers to reduce responsibilities of beginning special educators • offers to reduce responsibilities of mentors • participates in evaluation of program		

SOURCE: White, M., & Mason, C. (2001). *Mentoring Induction Principles and Guidelines.* Retrieved October 2, 2002 from http://www.cec.sped.org/spotlight/udl/mip_g_manual_11pt.pdf. Reprinted with permission.

94

Designing Effective 5
Professional
Development

Before it can happen for students, it must first happen for teachers.

Linda Darling-Hammond

School and district leaders usually have little control over the preservice preparation of special educators. However, they can enhance the skills and quality of the teachers they hire (Local Administrators' Role in Promoting Teacher Quality, 2002).

Typical practices, such as the "sit and get" method in which experts present information are not associated with either changes in teacher behavior or student learning (Guskey, 2003; McLeskey & Waldron, 2002). In contrast, effective professional development practices are linked to increased teacher effectiveness, teacher efficacy, and student achievement (Hawley & Valli, 1999). Teachers who have well-structured opportunities to learn and develop their skills are more likely to experience job satisfaction and feel greater commitment to their work (Gersten et al., 2001). Developing strong professional development programs is an important leadership responsibility and requires thoughtful and systematic planning and needs to be a critical leadership priority.

SCENARIO: UNCLEAR BOUNDARIES

Zina, the special education director, talks informally with several principals after a meeting. The conversation moves to professional development plans for the upcoming school year. Hannah, a high school principal, says she involves special education teachers in professional development sessions with all teachers. However, she suggests there are some unique professional development needs for special educators that aren't being adequately addressed. Hannah is particularly concerned about the new teacher they hired to coteach who hasn't yet finished her special education teacher preparation program. Hannah asks Zina, "Isn't it your responsibility to assist the teacher with specific training needs?" Dennis, an elementary principal, discusses the struggle both general and special education teachers experience as they have moved to greater inclusion of students with disabilities. He doesn't think the consultant that they hired last year was very helpful. Hannah nods and states she doesn't know enough to help teachers with inclusion issues. Zina listens, realizing that they need to work more closely together to identify needs and plan effective professional development for both general and special educators.

CHAPTER OVERVIEW

The purpose of this chapter is not to comprehensively address the topic of professional development, but to address the specific needs of teachers as they work with students with disabilities. This chapter addresses:

- Involving teachers in assessing needs and planning goals,
- Using effective professional development practices,
- Clarifying leader roles in professional development,
- Developing school-university partnerships for professional development, and
- Enhancing experienced teachers' professional growth.

INVOLVE TEACHERS IN ASSESSING NEEDS AND PLANNING GOALS

Professional development goals need to emerge from the needs of teachers. NCLB requires that professional development be planned with significant participation of principals, teachers, parents, and administrators (see Figure 5.1). Teachers need opportunities to define what it is they need to learn, and to have a say in learning processes. Such engagement increases the likelihood that what teachers learn will be relevant to their needs and also helps increase their motivation and commitment to learn (Hawley & Valli, 1999).

[from Title IX, Section 9101(34) statue]
The term "professional development" includes activities that:

- improve and increase teachers' knowledge of the academic subjects the teachers teach, and enable teachers to become highly qualified;
- are an integral part of broad schoolwide and districtwide educational improvement plans;
- give teachers, principals, and administrators the knowledge and skills to provide students with the opportunity to meet challenging State academic content and student academic achievement standards;
- improve classroom management skills;
- are high quality, sustained, intensive, and classroom focused in order to have a positive and lasting impact on classroom instruction and the teacher's performance in the classroom;
- support the recruiting, hiring, and training of highly qualified teachers, including teachers who became highly qualified through State and local alternative routes to certification;
- advance teacher understanding of effective instructional strategies that are based on scientifically based research;
- are aligned with and directly related to State academic content standards, student achievement standards, and assessments;
- are developed with extensive participation of teachers, principals, parents, and administrators of schools to be served under this Act;
- are designed to give teachers of limited English-proficient children the knowledge and skills to provide instruction and appropriate language and academic support services to those children, including the appropriate use of curricula and assessments;
- provide training for teachers and principals in the use of technology so that technology and technology applications are effectively used in the classroom to improve teaching and learning in the curricula and core academic subjects in which the teachers teach;
- are regularly evaluated for their impact on increased teacher effectiveness and improved student academic achievement, with the findings of the evaluations used to improve the quality of professional development;
- provide instruction in methods of teaching children with special needs;
- include instruction in the use of data and assessments to inform and instruct classroom practice; and
- include instruction in ways that teachers, principals, pupil services personnel, and school administrators may work more effectively with parents.

Figure 5.1   Professional Development Definition From NCLB

Address Special Educators' Unique Needs

Although special and general education teachers need joint professional development opportunities, special educators do have unique needs. Leaders should ask special educators to describe goals for their own learning and how they would like to accomplish these goals. Sometimes the learning goals of special educators may be very specific and require the use of resources outside the district. This is particularly true of teachers who teach students with low-incidence disabilities (e.g., vision and hearing impairments, severe disabilities). Both school and district leaders can assess needs through discussions, surveys, and through planning teams. In particular, district leaders should analyze special educators' needs across the district through mail or electronic surveys and analyze the needs of specific teacher groups (e.g., low-incidence versus high-incidence teachers, experienced versus new teachers). School and district leaders need to work to coordinate their professional development efforts for teachers.

Assess Teachers' Needs for Working in Inclusive and Collaborative Settings

NCLB specifically addresses the need for professional development to help teachers instruct special needs children. A recent study shows that 96% of students with disabilities are taught in regular school buildings by general educators ("General Education Teachers' Role," 2001). The physical inclusion of students with disabilities in general education classrooms is not a sufficient goal: Teachers must be ready and willing to differentiate instruction for students so they can have "cognitive access" to the general education curriculum (Little & Houston, 2003).

Teachers need to have opportunities to raise questions and have a range of needs addressed in professional development. The knowledge base will not necessarily provide all of the answers, because teachers face ethical, moral, and practical issues in changing their practices (Bondy & Brownell, 2004). Teachers need to have more than just knowledge about practices, they need to be able to raise questions and discuss their concerns. For example:

- What is my role in inclusive programs?
- How will inclusion impact the academic and social progress of my other students?
- Will I have the time and resources to plan and implement a program? (McLeskey & Waldron, 2002).

Because inclusion differs across schools, grade levels, and subject areas, inclusive practices and specific professional development needs should be tailored to the needs of school (McLeskey & Waldron, 2002). Principals can assess teachers' needs by encouraging teams of teachers to discuss their concerns and describe their professional development needs.

USE EFFECTIVE PROFESSIONAL
DEVELOPMENT PRACTICES

Over the last two decades much has been learned about effective professional development practices and how to encourage the use of research-based practices in schools. NCLB recognizes the role that high-quality professional development plays in increasing achievement in schools and outlines specific criteria for professional development (see Figure 5.1).

These NCLB criteria are consistent with much that has been written about effective professional development practices (e.g., Guskey, 2003; National Staff Development Council, 2001). These criteria include advancing teachers' understanding of scientifically based research, aligning professional development with content standards, and evaluating the impact of professional development on student achievement.

Although a recent study suggests that special educators spend substantial time in professional development activities, these activities do not always reflect current knowledge about effective practices, such as engaging teachers in their own learning or allowing time to support the development of new skills (A High-Quality Teacher for Every Classroom, 2002).

The following recommendations for professional development are drawn from the special education research-to-practice literature (e.g., Gersten & Dimino, 2001; Klingner, Ahwee, Pilonieta, & Menendez, 2003) and research on professional development and change (e.g., Guskey, 2003; Hawley & Valli, 1999; The National Staff Development Council, 2001). Figure 5.2 provides a summary of facilitators and barriers to the use of evidence-based practices (Klingner, 2004).

Includes Research-Based Practices
That Focus on Student Achievement

Professional development should focus on improving student achievement. Selecting interventions for use in schools requires attention to research-based practices (i.e., educational practices that have been examined by the larger research community) that foster student achievement. There is an impressive amount of knowledge about effective special education teaching practices; however, this knowledge is often untapped by practitioners (Fuchs & Fuchs, 1998).

Teachers need encouragement and support to evaluate new teaching practices and to assess whether specific teaching behaviors are leading to improved student learning. Teachers are more motivated to use an

Facilitators
Ongoing Assistance and Support

Coaches and mentors to provide feedback, help problem solve, and provide assistance with learning the critical components of practices.
Opportunities to observe demonstrations of the practices.
Administrative support (e.g., clear expectations that practices are important, scheduled time for planning and implementation, help with resources, and a reward structure).
A community of practice (i.e., a network of teachers using the practices and who dialogue, help one another, and encourage risk taking).
Help with materials and other resources.

Positive Student Outcomes

Research results clearly linking enhanced student achievement with the practice.
Students' liking the practice.

Strong Relationships Among Researchers, Teachers, Administrators, and District Leaders

Relationships built over time on trust and mutual respect.
Open lines of communication.

"Buy-In"

Strong grassroots support from teachers, and time and space for participation to grow from year to year.
Teacher involvement in planning, providing feedback, and problem solving.
Transfer of ownership of the practices from researchers to teachers.
Buy-in by stakeholders at multiple levels (i.e., teachers, administrators, and district leaders).
Belief by teachers that they are learning cutting-edge instructional practices.

Barriers
Competing Demands

High-stakes testing (and pressure to engage in test-preparation activities).
Pressure to cover content ("breadth versus depth" [some instructional practices, such as comprehension strategy instruction, take longer than traditional methods]).
Time constraints (i.e., multiple demands on time).

Lack of Supports

Inadequate support from administrators.
Insufficient support from the researchers providing professional development.
Lack of appropriate materials (including published materials).
Mismatch between teacher's style or personality and the instructional practice.
Lacking an in-depth understanding of the practice and its critical components.
Forgetting to use a practice, or forgetting *how* to use it.

Figure 5.2   Facilitators and Barriers to the Sustained Use of Evidence-Based Practices

SOURCE: Klingner, J. K. (2004). The science of professional development. *Journal of Learning Disabilities, 37*(3), 248–255. Adapted with permission.

intervention when they see that it leads to academic achievement in their students (Gersten, Vaughn, Deshler, & Schiller, 1997).

Takes Place in Collaborative Learning Communities

Creating strong professional development programs is easier in schools where *ongoing* learning is a part of the school culture. Strong professional learning communities are organized to support collaboration and learning around problems of practice (Johnson & Birkeland, 2003b). In learning communities, professional development is "owned" by teachers (National Staff Development Council, 2001). Teachers work together as mutual learners and leaders in study groups, learning-focused staff meetings, and action-research teams. Participants work together, observe each other, dialogue, network, and share their thought processes (Lambert, 2002). In learning communities, professional development and change are an integral part of the daily life of the school (National Staff Development Council, 2001).

Collaborative communities are not easy to establish; they take time and they require leader support. School leaders can encourage collaborations that focus on student learning and teaching practice, and provide structures that allow teachers to discuss and analyze student work. When engaged in the larger learning community, special educators both contribute to and benefit from their general education colleagues' expertise.

Meets the "Reality" Principle

The "reality" principle suggests that if professional development is to be useful to teachers, research must be translated into manageable, concrete, and comprehensive teaching strategies and procedures (Gersten & Dimino, 2001). Many professional development efforts fail because they are impractical, lack specificity, and try to do too much at once (Hawley & Valli, 1999). Teachers need specific guidelines, examples, and procedures to increase the likelihood that new approaches will be implemented.

New teaching strategies also need to "fit" within the structure of classrooms (Gersten & Dimino, 2001, p. 122). Teachers indicate they are willing to use new approaches and make accommodations for students with disabilities, provided that the new practices also help other students in the classroom (Vaughn, Hughes, Schumm, & Klingner, 1998).

Includes a Conceptual Component

Professional development programs need to include a conceptual component that helps teachers understand how new instructional approaches differ from those they have used and to understand why they are better (Gersten & Dimino, 2001). Teachers often initially express concern about using new procedures. Teachers who comprehend the underlying purposes of new approaches are able to use and adapt them with greater confidence (Hawley & Valli, 1999).

Provides Opportunities for Coaching and Technical Assistance

Teachers need to learn about new innovations and apply new knowledge in their own classrooms and receive feedback and assistance from those knowledgeable in the intervention (Gersten et al., 1997). As Sandy explains after a professional development experience:

> You did a good job in showing me and modeling a lesson for me. It was good, but when I would try something then I would again teach like, "What happens in this case?," because once you start doing this you have more questions. I felt like they were maybe simple little questions but if I don't have the answers I don't feel comfortable with what I'm doing, and then it just doesn't work for me (Klingner et al., 2003, p. 422).

Teachers are motivated to incorporate an intervention into their daily routines after they have had success with the intervention. Therefore, it is critical to address teachers' questions and provide support during implementation.

CLARIFY LEADERS' ROLES IN PROFESSIONAL DEVELOPMENT

The above guidelines suggest that new instructional practices need to be systematically introduced, that teachers understand specifically how to use these practices, why the practices are important, and when they are appropriate. Teachers need to understand the conceptual foundations of the practice and have opportunities to implement the practice in their classrooms while receiving follow-up coaching and feedback. Teachers who are learning these practices need to be able to discuss problems and barriers to using the practice, as well as be given opportunities to network with others who use the practice (Klingner et al., 2003).

The Role of Principal Support in Professional Development

Although teachers are asked to learn new instructional approaches, the work environment is often not organized to support the use of the new practices (Hawley & Valli, 1999). One of the most important facilitators to implementing new practices is principal support. Principals can show their support in a number of ways, such as:

- Helping to create a school culture that values professional learning and collaboration;
- Showing an interest in teachers' learning and in research-based practices;
- Encouraging the use of practices learned through professional development;
- Providing resources, time, and follow-up needed to implement and sustain new practices;
- Encouraging teachers to adjust the instructional practices to work in their settings;
- Providing teachers with feedback about their practices; and
- Limiting requests for teachers to participate in other competing professional development activities while they are establishing new practices (Klingner, 2004; Klingner et al., 2003).

The Role of District Leaders in Professional Development

When district administrators partner with principals in meeting the professional development needs of special educators, it eliminates redundancy and reduces the burden on school leaders. District leaders are also in a position to support school professional development efforts through garnering resources, helping plan professional development programs, and taking responsibility for districtwide professional development needs. Some district professional development experiences are helpful because special educators welcome opportunities to collaborate with their peers in other schools, especially if there is time to exchange ideas, observe each other, and share experiences. For teachers of students with low-incidence disabilities, using electronic resources, such as Web sites and teacher listservs, is critical to connect with teachers outside the district who have special expertise.

DEVELOPING UNIVERSITY-SCHOOL PARTNERSHIPS FOR PROFESSIONAL DEVELOPMENT

School and district leaders should consider university-school partnerships for professional development. NCLB explicitly recognizes the benefits of school and university partnerships to prepare and support teachers. Collaborative partnerships between schools and universities can enhance teachers' professional development by involving those with varied expertise and sharing resources to meet mutually defined goals. These collaborations may be formal or informal. Regardless of the degree of structure involved, they need to be designed with the guidelines for effective professional development in mind.

Professional Development Schools

Professional development schools (PDS) provide school leaders and teachers with opportunities to influence both teacher preparation and to enhance the development of practicing teachers. These PDS partnerships are formal arrangements, similar to teaching hospitals, which bring teachers and school leaders together with university faculty to improve teaching and learning (Rice & Afman, 2002).

Some evidence suggests that PDS partnerships may boost teacher retention rates and can help develop high-quality alternate routes into teaching (Pritchard & Ancess, 1999). Specifically, PDS partnerships are designed to achieve four major goals:

1. Prepare teachers,

2. Increase student achievement,

3. Provide professional development for teachers, and

4. Encourage inquiry about teaching and learning (NCATE, 2004).

These formal PDS arrangements enhance the professional development opportunities of both university and school participants by providing opportunities to collaborate, share resources, and link teacher preparation to the everyday life of schools. University and school faculty jointly work in public schools to supervise preservice teachers, engage in professional development, problem solve, team teach, and engage in action research (NCATE, 2004).

Although PDSs have grown from 100 to more than 1,000 today (Rice, 2002), the role of PDSs in special education is less developed and refined (Voltz, 2001). PDSs have the potential to bring together general and special education faculty from universities and schools to collaborate to serve all students' needs.

PDS partnerships must be characterized by reciprocity and parity for both university and school partners. These relationships emerge over time and initially focus on establishing relationships, mutual values, and understandings. They eventually move toward a formal partnership in which both the school and university share responsibilities (Frampton, Vaughn, & Didelot, 2003). Rice (2002) suggests five recommendations for developing PDS partnerships:

1. PDSs must be *voluntary* endeavors, and initiated through invitation rather than mandate.

2. A *shared vision of the PDS* needs to be established at the beginning of the partnership.

3. Activities are needed to *establish trust* among the participants of the PDS, which include informal meetings and social gatherings.

4. A plan is needed for *funding the PDS*, considering how both the use of outside resources and funding will be sustained over time.

5. *Written policies* that specify how the PDS will operate are needed to facilitate communication and collaboration among participants.

If PDSs are to thrive, school leaders must be supportive of the partnerships (Frampton et al., 2003). There are few descriptions of PDS schools that involve special education teachers. Lisa Hess, who has been involved in a PDS effort in educating students with emotional disorders, describes below what it is like to work in a PDS school.

Personal Perspective: Working in a Professional Development School

Elizabeth Hess Rice*

What is it like to work in a Professional Development School? Many cases studies have sought to illustrate the stress and strains as well as the joys and benefits of a school-university collaboration. Standards have been written, research has been "conducted," but the question remains. . . . *What is it really like?*

In order to answer this question I keep asking myself, "With whose voice should I speak?" There are so many voices and perspectives in a true PDS—a cacophony of voices that both help improve practice and make the process so confusing. The results are difficult to measure. Each partner gives so much and "dances" all year between systems and needs.

If I were writing this from the perspective of a cooperating teacher I might tell you how exciting yet how difficult it is to "talk through" each step of my thinking process with graduate students. If I were a graduate student I might talk about how tired I am with the pace of teaching during the day and taking classes in the evenings. If I were a site administrator I might talk to you about how wonderful it is to have extra hands but how difficult it is to live through the learning curve of new interns every year. If I were a student in K–8th grade I might tell you how hard it is for me to see interns come and go every year but how happy I am that there are more people available to me.

In Programs for Teaching Students with Emotional and Behavioral Disabilities (EBD) at the George Washington University we have two professional development schools: (1) The Marshall Road Professional Development School with Fairfax County, Virginia, and (2) The Children's Guild Professional Development School with The Children's Guild in Chillum, Maryland. In these schools we have a university faculty member, three university supervisors and staff, four site administrators, eight special education cooperating teachers, a myriad of general educators, many district supporters, the university administration, sixteen graduate interns yearly, and approximately 100 K–8 students with emotional and behavioral disabilities. We are all in constant contact. We e-mail. We talk on the phone late at night. We revisit the same problems we had last year (e.g., Is this novice teacher gaining the needed skills at an adequate rate? Is the cooperating teacher really using strength-based interventions and giving our students the model they need? Will our budget be approved this year?) We also encounter new challenges (e.g., Is this site administrator really leaving this year? Are we mislabeling a K–8 student because we are "tired" of his or her behavior? How can we make our program more inclusive?). Site administrators are adjunct faculty. Our graduates become cooperating teachers. We are enmeshed.

The process of working in a PDS is truly exhausting, especially in the early spring when all teachers are struggling with paperwork, district mandates, and the regressive needs of troubled students during this time. We, like many educators ask ourselves: Are we really reaching and teaching our K–8 students? Do our graduate teaching interns have the skills and dispositions needed to teach troubled kids? Are we burning our cooperating teachers out? Are we addressing the needs of the whole child? Is all this work worth it? Do the school and university systems value our work? And yet . . . we continue.

We've been continuing and "getting better at getting better" for 10 years now. Why? Because we are part of a team of university and school professionals who are influencing K–8 and graduate students on a daily basis. As a faculty member, I am not just talking about teaching students with EBD. I am living it from multiple perspectives. We are energized by our work together in this young, and often misunderstood, field.

---

*Dr. Elizabeth Hess Rice is an assistant professor at George Washington University in Washington, D.C.

Examples of District- and Statewide Partnerships

Project PREPARE

Project PREPARE, a five-year school-university partnership, used effective professional development practices to support underperforming rural elementary and primary schools. The project included:

- Collaborative structures for professional development with the purpose of improving student achievement,
- Consultation services and material supports to assist with changes initiated by the district, and
- Leadership to help the district with long-term systemic change (Mariage & Garmon, 2003).

The PREPARE project incorporates a model of professional development based on effective practices to guide the change efforts and included six voluntary structures including a model summer school program, teacher study groups, home-school partnerships, a mentor/intern program, a mentor/mentee program, and a professional development center. For example, the model school program is designed to provide new and experienced teachers with opportunities to work with the lowest-performing students during a seven-week summer program. Summer school was preceded by a one-week professional development program, and teachers worked to provide literacy and math instruction in collaborate teams, with a faculty member, a graduate student, and a paraprofessional.

During the course of the PREPARE project, there were steady improvements in student achievement in reading and mathematics on multiple measures, including state-mandated criterion-referenced tests (Mariage & Garmon, 2003).

Project CENTRAL

Another example of a school-district partnership is Project CENTRAL (Coordinating Existing Networks to Reach All Learners). This state-funded program was developed to identify and disseminate research-based instructional practices through professional development in Florida (Little & Houston, 2003). A conceptual model was designed to deliver a continuous improvement plan to increase the achievement of students with and without disabilities. The following four steps are part of the model:

1. Identify research-based practices.

2. Select a team to attend awareness-level professional development sessions.

3. Implement research-based instructional practices from initial training.

4. Collect data on the results of student learning through action research and traditional methods.

The model includes planning, coaching, action research, and support for each initiative. Evaluation results showed high levels of implementation, changes in student behavior, and participant satisfaction (Little & Houston, 2003).

ENHANCING EXPERIENCED TEACHERS' PROFESSIONAL GROWTH

Experienced special educators need professional development opportunities to continue to develop their expertise and skills and to avoid the withdrawal and stagnation that sometimes occurs after years in the classroom. School communities that emphasize high expectations for all students and provide collaborative and ongoing opportunities for professional development help to facilitate teachers' professional growth and renewal. This section addresses challenging experienced and accomplished teachers through National Board Certification and teacher leadership opportunities.

National Board Certification

Principals should encourage highly motivated special educators to pursue the National Board Teacher Certificate (see Chapter 3 for a description). The National Board for Professional Teaching Standards (NBPTS) recognizes accomplished teachers, and promotes National Board Certification as a platform for school improvement and as a method of providing teacher-leaders. Although no specific evidence is available about National Board Certification and retention in special education, a recent report suggests many National Board-Certified teachers (NBCTs) stay in teaching and most of the others remain in the field in some capacity ("National Boards Set Standards," 2004).

Earning National Board Certification enhances teacher quality. A recent study suggests that NBCTs consistently demonstrated a higher level of expertise on all thirteen attributes of exemplary teaching ("A Distinction That Matters," 2004). Special educators who have earned the "Exceptional Needs Certificate" indicate that it was the most valuable professional experience that they have had. Many of these nationally certified teachers serve as mentors for others ("National Board Sets Standards," 2004).

Applicants should expect to spend 200 to 400 hours to earn certification. Much of the work is directed at analyzing and reflecting on their teaching practices, how their work influences the learning of their students, and how they support diverse students. As Jane Humphrey, the Council for Exceptional Children's 2003 Clarissa Hug Teacher of the Year states,

> [Certification] has helped me as a teacher, because the year I worked on certification, I internalized the standards, and I continue to apply them each day in my classroom and in daily reflections on what happened with the students ("National Boards Set Standards," 2004, p. 5).

Cynthia Evans, another Exceptional Needs specialist, states:

> This process has been of immense benefit to me as well as to my students. The entire process has altered the way I teach. I found the creation of my portfolio demanded much in terms of analysis and reflection on my teaching practices. I questioned my own ideas and methods, which led to the application of innovative approaches, which at the same time allowed me to recognize that which was good in what I did ("A Distinction That Matters," 2004).

The cost of the National Board Certification is $2,300; the certificate is valid for ten years and is renewable. Because of the costs, states and districts need to assist teachers by covering some or all of the certification expenses. Another possibility for funding is through the use of NCLB funds (see Potential Sources of Federal Funds Identified for National Board Certification at http://www/nbpts.org/about/govt.cfm).

Administrators can support and encourage special educators to pursue National Board Certification by:

- Publicizing incentives and providing information about National Board Certification,
- Encouraging teachers to use online support groups and candidate partners,
- Suggesting the use of resources provided by the NBCTP Web site,
- Establishing local incentives such as recognition and new teacher leadership roles,
- Supporting candidates by paying or at least partially reimbursing the $2,300 assessment fee, and
- Providing specific compensation for achievement on the salary scale ("A Distinction That Matters," 2004).

Teacher Leadership as Professional Development

Providing teachers with opportunities to serve as leaders and make career advancements may help to attract and retain highly qualified teachers. There are many avenues for sharing leadership with teachers. Principals can provide teachers with opportunities to participate in important decisions such as teacher hiring, professional development, developing curricula, and determining the school budget.

Providing "master teacher" status recognizes accomplished special educators and allows them to use their expertise in new ways. Teacher leaders often have additional responsibilities, higher salaries to compensate them for their differentiated "master teacher" positions, and opportunities to influence education beyond their own classrooms. For example, the Teacher Advancement Program implemented in Arizona and supported by the Milken Family Foundation, provides new career paths, increased salaries, and new responsibilities for their most talented teachers (see http://www.azcentral.com/arizonarepublic/local/articles/0408shining-teach08.html).

Mentoring is another form of leadership that encourages experienced special educators to share what they have learned, to engage in professional development, and to reflect on their own practices. Mentors learn how to observe and give feedback, help other teachers grow, and become more attuned to the needs of new teachers in their schools (Moir & Bloom, 2003). Experienced teachers might serve in a number of different roles including model teachers, mentor coordinators, team leaders, and in-class coaches (Johnson & Kardos, 2002).

TIPS FOR LEADERS

Evaluate the School and District Professional Development Programs

Evaluate how well the school and district are using effective professional development practices. A new Assessment Inventory is available from the National Staff Development Council. The 60-item inventory is designed to assess school and district's professional development (more information on effective practices and the inventory is available at http://www.nsdc.org).

Keep Teachers Informed of Research-Based Practices

Leaders can keep special educators informed of new developments in the field by:

- Providing monthly newsletters and/or e-mail announcements about relevant courses, Web sites, professional meetings, and resource materials;
- Creating a professional library with journals, books, and videos;
- Providing special educators opportunities to visit and observe other teachers;
- Providing funds for all teachers to join the professional organization of their choice;
- Sending teachers to a conference with others who do similar work;
- Providing districtwide area meetings for special educators with similar expertise (e.g., speech-language pathologists); and
- Encouraging teachers to take courses to continue to develop their expertise.

Encourage Teachers to Join Professional Organizations

Being part of a professional organization keeps teachers connected to a larger community. Leaders can encourage such memberships by funding part or all of a membership of the teacher's choice, and by supporting teachers' attendance at professional conferences.

SUMMARY

- Professional development has the potential to increase teacher quality and teacher retention.
- Both school and district leaders have responsibilities to coordinate professional development efforts using effective practices.
- Teachers are more likely to make changes in their teaching practices when provided with well-designed professional development programs, ongoing assistance and coaching, and administrative support.
- Special and general education teachers need professional development opportunities that help them meet the needs of students with disabilities in their classrooms.
- School-university collaborations promote shared responsibility for the professional development of experienced and new teachers through formal collaborations, such as PDS schools and other informal agreements.
- Although current reform efforts focus heavily on induction and professional development for new teachers, experienced teachers also need ongoing opportunities to learn and serve in leadership roles.

SELECTED READINGS

Gersten, R., & Dimino, J. (2001). The realities of translating research into classroom practice. *Learning Disabilities Research & Practice, 16,* 120–130.

Rice, E. H. (2002). The collaboration process in professional development schools: Results of a meta-ethnology, 1990–1998. *Journal of Teacher Education, 53*(1), 55–67.

Klingner, J. K., Ahwee, S., Pilonieta, P., & Menendez, R. (2003). Barriers and facilitators in scaling up research-based practices. *Exceptional Children, 69*(4), 411–429.

Little, M. E., & Houston, D. (2003). Research into practice through professional development. *Remedial and Special Education, 24*(2), 75–87.

Mariage, T. V., & Garmon, M. A. (2003). A case of educational change: Improving student achievement through a school-university partnership. *Remedial and Special Education, 24*(4), 215–234.

McLeskey, J., & Waldron, N. L. (2002). Professional development and inclusive schools: Reflections on effective practice. *The Teacher Educator, 37*(3), 159–173.

WEB SITES

Council for Exceptional Children (CEC)

http://www.cec.sped.org/ps/

The CEC Web site provides information on the National Council for Accreditation of Teacher Education (NCATE) standards for special education and provides many professional development opportunities and resources.

National Board for Professional Teaching Standards (NBPTS)

http://www.nbpts.org

NBPTS is an independent, nonprofit, nonpartisan organization offering advanced certification for teachers.

National Staff Development Council (NSDC)

http://www.nsdc.org/standards/collaborationskills.cfm

The NSDC is a nonprofit professional association committed to ensuring student success through staff development and school improvement.

Professional Development Links (North Central Regional Educational Laboratory)

http://www.ncrel.org/info/pd/

This Web site contains links and documents of relevance for those interested in providing strong professional development programs.

Part III

Creating Positive Work Environments

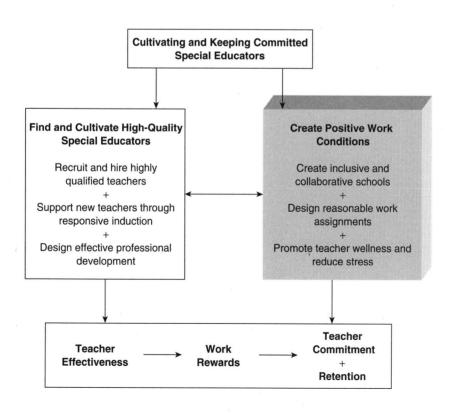

Cultivating and Keeping Committed Special Educators

Find and Cultivate High-Quality Special Educators

Recruit and hire highly qualified teachers
+
Support new teachers through responsive induction
+
Design effective professional development

Create Positive Work Conditions

Create inclusive and collaborative schools
+
Design reasonable work assignments
+
Promote teacher wellness and reduce stress

Teacher Effectiveness → Work Rewards → Teacher Commitment + Retention

Creating Inclusive and Collaborative Schools   **6**

"Sometimes just knowing the principal is supportive and there to help makes a difference. As one teacher stated, the important thing was not always getting what they requested, but rather 'in feeling that someone was out there advocating for her needs.'"

(Guzman, 1997, p. 5)

Principals' actions as school leaders make a major difference in what special educators accomplish in their schools and what students with disabilities achieve. Principals help prevent attrition by creating positive work environments for teachers and fostering the development of strong teaching and learning environments for students.

Special education teachers are concerned both with providing specially designed instruction that meets the individual needs of their students and ensuring that students with disabilities have access to the general education curriculum. Because most students with disabilities are served in regular education classes for at least part of the school day, principals need to facilitate collaboration among general and special educators who share in the responsibility for educating these students.

SCENARIO: WHAT A DIFFERENCE A PRINCIPAL CAN MAKE

Two special educators see each other for the first time in six years at a state education conference. Johanna describes her teaching career with excitement. She talks about her students, what they are accomplishing, and the great principal and colleagues at her school. She describes a coteaching effort that was initiated at her school and is now being modeled at other schools. She is continuing to learn and is optimistic about her work. Ann listens, wishing she felt the same way. But she feels isolated; her work is misunderstood by the principal and her colleagues. Ann states, "my principal can't be bothered about many things that are important in this school. His usual response to my needs is to call Fred [the special education director]. Fred isn't the principal and he can't help me with some of the problems in my job." Ann feels stagnant and is beginning to think that she will never be effective in her school. As they continue to share, it becomes evident that Johanna is supported in her work in ways that Ann is not.

The Importance of Principal Support

- Teachers who stay in their positions are almost four times more likely than those who leave to strongly perceive administrators' behavior as supportive and encouraging (Boe, Barkanic, & Leow, 1999).
- Special educators indicate that the top-rated incentive for staying in special education is a supportive principal (Schnorr, 1995).
- Principal support offers benefits beyond teacher retention. Supported teachers are more likely than their less-supported colleagues to report:
  - Job satisfaction,
  - Commitment to their work,
  - Greater colleague support,
  - Fewer role problems, and
  - Less stress and burnout (Billingsley, 2004; Gersten et al., 2001).

CHAPTER OVERVIEW

The goal of this chapter is to highlight those specific leadership supports that are necessary to create a supportive climate for special and general educators and the work conditions necessary for teachers to accomplish their goals in inclusive schools. Specifically, principals can foster inclusive and collaborative schools by attending to eight key leadership tasks:

- Providing a welcoming and emotionally supportive environment,
- Advocating for full educational opportunities for all students,
- Assuring access to the general curriculum,
- Fostering collaborative relationships,
- Facilitating the development of individualized education programs (IEPs),

- Ensuring appropriate assessments for students with disabilities,
- Helping special educators assess their effectiveness, and
- Facilitating shared leadership and decision making.

EIGHT LEADERSHIP TASKS FOR INCLUSIVE AND COLLABORATIVE SCHOOLS

Figure 6.1 highlights eight leadership supports that are necessary for creating collaborative and inclusive schools. The questions outlined in Figure 6.1 can be used to consider the extent to which these supports are provided in schools. These questions may also be used as prompts to generate discussion among faculty.

Figure 6.1 Leadership Support for Inclusive and Collaborative Schools

Key Forms of Support:	Questions to Consider:
Provides a welcoming and emotionally supportive environment	• Are all students, families, and their teachers made to feel welcome in schools and classrooms? • Are special educators treated as part of the entire school team? • Do all teachers, students, and families feel a sense of belonging in the school? • Are interactions based on an ethic of care and respect? • Do special educators and students with disabilities participate in school activities (e.g., field trips, programs)? • What efforts are given to establishing relationships and communicating with itinerant personnel in the school (e.g., part-time special educators, psychologists, related-services personnel)?
Advocates for full educational opportunities for all students	• Is there a written school mission that addresses the needs of all students? • Does the principal communicate the importance of serving all students to school staff and external audiences? • Are the principal and school staff aware of the key principles underlying IDEA? • Do teachers, paraprofessionals, and other support staff understand their roles in the education of students with disabilities? • Are they clear about others' roles?
Ensures access to the general education curriculum	• Is access to the general education curriculum considered in educational planning? • Do teachers take time to understand the needs of students with disabilities in their classes? • Do teams recognize the need for individual considerations in educating students with disabilities? • Is access to extended curriculum provided as needed? • Are instruction and supports sufficient to ensure progress?

(Continued)

Figure 6.1 (Continued)

Key Forms of Support:	Questions to Consider:
Fosters collaborative relationships	• Is the school climate characterized by collegiality, shared decision making, and a shared responsibility for school goals? • Do members of the school community work together to plan, problem solve, and share resources? • Does everyone understand the need for and goals of collaboration to serve the needs of students with disabilities? • Is there an understanding of teachers, and paraprofessionals' roles in collaboration? • Do teachers and paraprofessionals have the knowledge and skills needed to perform these roles? • Is time set aside for regular collaboration to occur?
Facilitates the development of Individualized Education Programs (IEPs)	• Are sufficient resources provided to meet the individual needs of students (e.g., specialized curriculum, intensive instructional support, technological supports, transition services, and related services)? • Do general educators participate in IEP meetings? • Are parents invited to be equal participants in IEP development? • Do teachers, paraprofessionals, and administrators understand the IEP process? • How do principals support the IEP process?
Ensures appropriate assessments for students with disabilities	• Are ongoing student assessments used to monitor students' progress and inform instructional decisions? • Are most students included in mandated assessments? • Are appropriate testing accommodations and alternative assessments available as needed?
Helps special educators assess how they are doing	• Do special educators have clear understandings of their roles in the school? • Are guidelines for effective practices understood? • Do special educators receive feedback about their work?
Facilitates shared leadership and decision making	• Do teachers have opportunities to participate in decisions that affect their daily work? • Is there an atmosphere of trust and openness so teachers can share issues and concerns? • Do teachers have opportunities for leadership?

Note: Leadership supports were identified from the following sources: Bateman & Bateman, 2001; Billingsley, Bodkins, & Hendricks, 1993; Burrello, Lashley, & Beatty, 2001; Crockett, 2002; DiPaola & Walther-Thomas, 2003; The ERIC/OSEP Special Project, 2002; Goor, Schwenn, & Boyer, 1997; Guzman, 1997; Lashley & Boscardin, 2003; National Association of Elementary School Principals & ILIAD Project, 2001.

Provides a Welcoming and Emotionally Supportive Environment

What principals say and do shows others what they value. Principals who treat students with disabilities, their families, and their teachers as valued members of the school recognize the school's role in serving students with disabilities. Welcoming students with disabilities, explicitly recognizing the role of schools in serving these students, helps to set the stage for teachers, parents, and students to feel a part of the school community.

Providing emotional support is an important part of creating an environment in which people feel valued. Emotional support is about availability, caring, and fostering relationships based on consideration, trust, and mutual respect. Cyndi Pitonyak provides a description of how her principal, Ray VanDyke, supports special and general educators at Kipps Elementary (see "Celebrating a Transformational Leader"). Her description of Ray includes numerous examples of emotional support.

Celebrating a Transformational Leader

*Cyndi Pitonyak**

Ray VanDyke has been an elementary principal for 18 years. His current school, Kipps Elementary, is an inclusive neighborhood school within the Montgomery County Public School District in the mountains of rural southwest Virginia. Kipps Elementary has received many national honors as a highly innovative and progressive school.[§]

I have worked with Ray for over 10 years. He is usually the last principal his teachers work with in our district, because it is extremely unusual for anyone to transfer out of Kipps Elementary. Teachers who work with Ray tend to leave only to relocate or to retire. I have been asked to consider what Ray does as an instructional leader to develop and sustain this school culture, which is innovative and growth oriented, and attracts and retains strong and committed teachers.

We have a strong sense of mission and identity in our work at Kipps Elementary. We know who we are and what we stand for as a school community. Time is spent talking about what we believe, and we examine our practices regularly to assess whether we are "walking our talk." This sense of mission and identity isn't handed down to us by Ray. Rather, it has *developed over time from the many opportunities* he creates for us to examine how we feel about our work and to evaluate what we are doing and where we are going. These opportunities include:

- Short discussions at faculty meetings,
- Voluntary book groups (that he actually attends!),
- Faculty retreats where we share what we are doing with each other and examine new ideas together,
- End-of-the-year "What have we accomplished and what do we want to work toward?" gatherings, and
- The many committees of teachers who collectively form the school's decision-making structure.

It is impossible for a teacher to just "go with the program" without self-examination or commitment for very long at Kipps Elementary. Day-to-day operations are organized in ways that require us to do our work collaboratively and with intention. Teachers feel empowered at Kipps, and Ray constantly notices, recognizes, and celebrates our successes in a spirit that fosters collective pride rather than competition. For many years he had a quote posted by his office door which read, "I am their leader, I must hasten after them."

But participatory decision making, community collaboration, and teacher empowerment are only part of the picture, and probably not even the most important part. As a human being, Ray absolutely *personifies the values* that are the most important elements of this healthy school climate. When asked why they love working at Kipps Elementary, my colleagues give reasons such as these:

"Ray treats me as a person, not a position."

"There isn't a big distance between Ray and us."

"Ray loves the kids and sees the humor and meaning in what we do every day, and he helps us see it when we forget."

"Ray doesn't take control and try to solve our problems for us."

"Ray trusts us."

Notice that these comments are all about Ray. We have developed a child-centered culture because Ray is child centered; we treat each other with respect because Ray models that with each and every one of us every single day; we ask each other for advice because Ray asks us for advice; we honor confidences because our confidences are honored; we help each other in difficult times because Ray helps us in difficult times; we get excited about new ideas because Ray is constantly sharing new ideas that he is excited about; we confront problems honestly and we look for solutions because we see Ray do this every day, for himself and with us— again and again, over time.

One colleague used the following metaphor to describe Ray's leadership:

> It's like Ray is standing at the door of the school each morning, whistling a tune. We all come in with our various moods and baggage and stresses and we just rush by. We hardly notice him, as he stands there whistling. But by the time we leave at the end of the day, each one of us walks out the door whistling that same tune. I don't know how he does it, but his spirit is contagious.

> Participatory decision making and collaborative school culture development are common aspirations for many public schools, but transformational leadership is the element that gives life and meaning to those aspirations. A quote widely attributed to Gandhi is "be the change you wish to see." Ray VanDyke is a classic example of a transformational leader who is a living example of the clear-eyed solutions he proposes.

---

*Cyndi Pitonyak is a special educator, Montgomery County Public Schools.

§Ray VanDyke was the principal at Gilbert Linkous Elementary during the year that the Academy Award-winning documentary, *Educating Peter*, was filmed. The film is about Peter, a child with Down syndrome, during his first year of being included in a third grade classroom.

Cyndi also describes how the emotional support that Ray provides serves as a model for how teachers treat each other in the school. "We treat each other with respect because Ray models that with each of us every single day."

Advocates for Full Educational Opportunities for All Students

A principal's major role is to help define and to communicate the school's educational mission (DiPaola & Walther-Thomas, 2003). Principals who advocate for full educational opportunity for students with disabilities set the stage for meeting individualized learning needs and help to promote equity and fairness under IDEA (Crockett, 2002). Advocating for students with disabilities means principals explicitly recognize the importance of serving these students and make this value clear to school staff and external audiences (DiPaola & Walthers Thomas, 2003).

Ideally, the principal helps shape the vision for special education in the school, and encourages students, teachers, and families to be part of developing written goals for special education. When the principal openly supports the education of all students, special educators are not the only voices advocating for students with disabilities, and both general and special educators are expected to share responsibility for students with disabilities.

Cyndi Pitonyak highlights the importance of a shared mission that was developed with faculty:

"We have a strong sense of mission and identity in our work."

"We know who we are and what we stand for as a school community."

"This sense of mission and identity isn't handed down to us by Ray. Rather, it has *developed over time from the many opportunities* he creates for us."

"Ray personifies the values that are the most important elements of this healthy school climate."

Ensures Access to the General Education Curriculum

Today the majority of students with disabilities spend at least part of their day in general education classrooms (McLaughlin & Nolet, 2004). Physical access to general education environments is insufficient for students with disabilities—they must have access to appropriate educational programs and services.

Students with disabilities need access to the general education curriculum (Individuals with Disabilities Education Act, 1997) as well as opportunities to meet the achievement standards developed by each state (No Child Left Behind, 2001). Teachers and administrators are often confused about what access means for students with disabilities and what this implies for teachers' work. This confusion can lead to hastily adopted policies or practices that ignore the needs of some students with disabilities.

Schools face unprecedented pressure to make sure that all (or most) students with disabilities meet state standards and pass district- and statewide assessments. The state standards required by NCLB can create conflicts for educators in deciding what to teach, what makes sense for

IEPs, and how to assess progress. Special educators are under pressure to ensure that their students meet prescribed standards. Consequently, they may feel pressure to teach standards that are inappropriate for a child at that point in time.

Although there is a need to provide students with disabilities appropriate access to general education, schools must continue to safeguard the need for *individual* considerations in educational planning (Crockett, 2002). Although the general education curriculum is a frame of reference for educational planning for students with disabilities, students' learning goals and objectives must be based on an analysis of each student's needs, with input from parents and students. Although many students with disabilities may have a curriculum that looks much like those of students without disabilities, other students will have more extensive needs that require alternative curriculum and assessments (McLaughlin & Nolet, 2004). It is also important to emphasize the importance of specialized services, supports, and accommodations to help students with disabilities meet important goals.

District and school leadership is critical to helping special and general educators address issues of general education curriculum access and individual planning. General and special educators need guidance through professional development opportunities, opportunities to raise questions and problem solve, as well as time to collaborate to address the needs of students with disabilities in their schools.

Fosters Collaborative Relationships

Because more students with disabilities are being included in general classes for instruction, special educators' roles are changing, with a greater emphasis on collaboration with general education teachers, paraprofessionals, and others involved with the child's well-being. Collaboration is needed to provide appropriate educational programs and to ensure that necessary modifications and adjustments are made for students with disabilities (Walther-Thomas, Korinek, McLaughlin, & Williams, 2000). Principals need to encourage collaborative relationships between general and special educators by encouraging dialogue, shared responsibilities, and professional development opportunities. Special educators who collaborate with others on a regular basis are not lone players with the primary responsibility for educating students with disabilities.

The purpose of collaboration is to determine the most "educationally enhancing learning environment" for each student and to ensure the availability of necessary supports (Idol, 1997, p. 384). An effective strategy for collaboration is to use *teams* of professionals and parents to make individual educational decisions. General educators who receive assistance from special educators are more confident in helping students with disabilities than general educators who do not receive such help (General Education Teachers' Role in Special Education, 2001).

Collaborative practices are easier to incorporate in schools where collegiality is the norm and where teachers routinely plan, work, and problem solve together. Collaboration assumes voluntary participation that is characterized by mutual goals; equality among those who participate; shared responsibility for participation, decision making, and outcomes; and shared resources (Friend & Cook, 2003). Teachers who have regular opportunities to collaborate together tend to bridge the boundaries of discipline and expertise (Lambert, 1998).

Special educators lack sufficient time to collaborate with their general education colleagues. Consider that "the majority of special educators report *they spend less than 1 hour per week in actual collaboration with colleagues*. What other profession requires collaboration yet allocates little to no time for it?" (Kozleski et al., 2000, p. 2).

Principals, therefore, need to facilitate collaborative practices by helping teachers develop the skills they need to collaborate effectively (e.g., communication skills, ways of teaching collaboratively) and to offer incentives for collaboration. They can also support teachers by helping them to clarify their roles in the collaborative process, and to ensure that teachers have time for collaboration (Idol, 1997). For more information on facilitating collaboration, see Chapter 7.

> **Improve Faculty Communication Through Web Site Communication**
>
> A school Web site site can be developed to "host a discussion board about areas of common interest or concern, to report on the work of different school committees, to post invitations to social gatherings, to share lesson ideas, to post articles and Web links that may be of interest to other teachers, or simply to exchange information about upcoming activities at school" (Brewster & Railsback, 2001, pp. 16-17).

Facilitates the Development of Individualized Education Programs (IEPs)

The above section addresses the importance of students' need to access the general education curriculum, while safeguarding students' rights for individualized considerations and support. The IEP outlines the goals of each student's program and shows where the student is "situated in the scope and sequence of the general education curriculum" (Nolet & McLaughlin, 2000, p. 22).

Principals need to be familiar with the legal requirements for the IEP, help facilitate the development of appropriate IEPs, and participate in IEP meetings when possible. The IEP committee has specific membership requirements, including a representative of the school district. The principal often fills this role. This district representative must be qualified to provide or supervise special education, be knowledgeable about the general education curriculum, and be authorized to commit school district resources.

Principal participation in IEP meetings has several benefits. Principals and teachers have opportunities to discuss issues of general education curriculum access, and discuss the child's needs with the parents and the other educators involved with the student. By being part of these conversations the principal will be aware of the staff and resources needed to implement the IEP. As one principal shares:

> A number of my principal colleagues ask me why I bother spending so much time in staffings. What I've learned is that many problems can be prevented when I know what's happening with these students. The time and energy spent in staffings pay dividends later on. Besides, I like to model what I believe is important (Guzman, 1997, p. 445).

When teachers understand the importance of high expectations for students with disabilities *and* the need for individualized decisions about curriculum and supports, students with disabilities will have greater opportunities to achieve important educational outcomes. Special education teachers will also work more effectively, since the basic assumptions of what special education is designed to provide are incorporated into the school culture.

Ensures Appropriate Assessments for Students With Disabilities

Teachers need to use ongoing assessments to monitor progress and determine when changes are needed in instruction (Fuchs, 2003). Curriculum-based measurements and assessments, portfolios, and mandated tests all provide data that can be used to assess current levels of performance and student progress. Teachers who continually assess students' progress toward goals are more likely to be effective and have concrete knowledge that their efforts are making a difference with students. Making a positive difference in the lives of students is an important factor in retention.

Helping general and special educators ensure appropriate state-mandated assessments and document-needed testing accommodations on the IEP are also a part of ensuring appropriate assessments. If students with disabilities do not participate in district- and statewide assessments, the IEP must include a statement indicating why the assessment is not appropriate and a description of the alternative achievement assessment. An excellent resource about assessment and testing accommodations for students with disabilities is the National Center on Educational Outcomes at www.education.umn.edu/nceo/

Helps Special Educators Assess Their Effectiveness

In the absence of feedback from others, special educators may experience unnecessary anxiety and wonder how the principal and others perceive their effectiveness. In the NCLB era of high-stakes testing, special educators may feel like they are ineffective when students do not meet the same standards as other students, even if these students have made significant progress. Parents may also express concerns when students do not pass mandated tests. This narrow sense of being unsuccessful in helping students meet mandated standards can create tension for teachers, especially if they are denied an opportunity to discuss these issues with school and district leaders. Because a large part of teachers' self-appraisal is associated with their students' progress, special educators may feel that they never accomplish enough.

School and district leaders have responsibilities to support special education teachers through feedback and evaluation. There are two major aspects of evaluation support. The first type of evaluation support provides teachers with *guidelines for self-assessment*. Teachers need to have guidelines against which their own behavior can be measured. If special educators are clear about their roles and responsibilities, understand their students' goals, and comprehend research-based practices, they can use these as guidelines to monitor their own activities and assess how they are doing.

The second type of evaluation is *informal or formal feedback from others*. Periodic observations and feedback from administrators and colleagues provide the teacher with opportunities to learn from others' analyses of their teaching. An annual review provides special educators with a global assessment of how they are doing, what worked well, and how they can continue to improve in meeting the individual needs of students with disabilities and helping students progress in the general education curriculum.

Facilitates Shared Leadership and Decision Making

As the above supports suggest, leadership for inclusive and collaborative schools is ideally shared among principals as well as general and special education teachers. Principals who empower general and special educators to collaborate and problem solve with student learning as the focus will promote a collective responsibility for students with disabilities in the school. This idea of developing leadership capacity among all members of the school community can positively influence how people will participate.

As Lambert (2002) states:

> Today's effective principal constructs a shared vision with members of the school community, convenes the conversations, insists on a student learning focus, evokes and supports leadership in others, models and participates in collaborative practices, helps pose the questions, and facilitates dialogue that addresses the confounding issues of practice. This work requires skill and new understanding; it is much easier to tell or to manage than it is to perform as a collaborative instructional leader (p. 40).

TIPS FOR LEADERS

The following tips are designed to improve the climate for special education teachers in the school and to encourage a work environment characterized by collegiality, respect, honesty, trust, and considerate behavior, all of which are at the core of positive working relationships.

Be Accessible

Accessible leaders have an open door policy, visit special educators' classes, return calls, and answer e-mails. Overall, special educators report fewer interactions with their principals than general educators, and are less likely to report that their principal understands what they do (Billingsley et al., 2004).

Listen to Special Education Teachers

Active listening requires principals to attend fully to teachers and to focus on what teachers are communicating. Principals who take time to listen to teachers have more opportunities to be supportive because they recognize their teachers' concerns and they understand what these teachers are trying to achieve.

A Special Educator's Perspective on Support

I've really had some great support from my district and from my school administrators. My district provides a lot of opportunities for professional development through inservices and meetings. But they also set aside funds for us to go to professional meetings and conferences. I know that's unusual for a district, but it helps so much, particularly because the special education field changes so rapidly. My principal and assistant principal both check in on me regularly, ask me how I'm doing, what I need . . . that sort of stuff. And, if I am having a problem, they work with me to solve it. They make a special effort towards my students, too (*Addressing the Revolving Door*, 2002).

Recognize Teachers' Accomplishments

It takes little effort recognize others' efforts and accomplishments. Encourage teachers by writing thank you notes, and taking time to notice what is going well. Recognize general and special educators' success in collaborating, in addressing difficult issues in IEP meetings, and in achieving success with their students.

Voice Support of Special Education Teachers and Students

Take time to emphasize the importance of serving all students during interviews, faculty meetings, and in communications with members of the community. Devote a faculty meeting to addressing the needs of students with disabilities in the school early in the year. Possible agenda items include inviting teachers to share issues and concerns, asking special educators to discuss current issues and developments in the field, and discussing professional development needs related to educating students with disabilities.

Keep Students With Disabilities at the Center of Conversations

Special educators sometimes complain that administrators are only concerned with meeting legal requirements and completing paperwork. Although school and district leaders must ensure compliance with state and federal laws, avoid letting these issues dominate conversations, meetings, and programs. Instead, keep students with disabilities at the heart of conversations and focus on what can be done to provide these students with what they need to be successful.

Encourage Relationship Building Among Special and General Educators

Relationships between special and general educators in the school are built by creating opportunities for teachers to communicate regularly and to interact about instructional issues and problems. Examples include the development of learning communities through collaboration, coteaching, networking, and joint professional development opportunities.

SUMMARY

- As school leaders, principals have an important responsibility to help create school environments in which all teachers can effectively do their work.
- Principals who advocate for all students in their schools by attending to critical leadership tasks demonstrate *support* for special education teachers, students with disabilities, and their families.
- Special educators who are supported by their principals are more likely to remain in special education teaching.
- Leadership for inclusive schools supports not just special educators, but all teachers working to meet the needs of students with disabilities.

SELECTED READINGS

Bateman, D., & Bateman, F. (2001). *A principal's guide to special education.* Arlington, VA: Council for Exceptional Children.

Burrello, L. C., Lashley, C., & Beatty, E. E. (2001). *Educating all students together: How school leaders create unified systems.* Thousand Oaks, CA: Corwin Press.

Council for Exceptional Children. (1999). *IEP team guide.* Arlington, VA.

Crockett, J. B. (2002). Special education's role in preparing responsive leaders for inclusive schools. *Remedial and Special Education, 23*(3), 157-168.

DiPaola, M. F., & Walther-Thomas, C. (2003). *Principals and special education: The critical role of school leaders* (No. COPSSE Document No. IB-7). Gainesville, FL: University of Florida, Center on Personnel Studies in Special Education.

The ERIC/OSEP Special Project. (2002). *To light a beacon: What administrators can do to make schools successful for all students.* ERIC/OSEP Topical Brief. Arlington, VA: The ERIC Clearinghouse on Disabilities and Gifted Education. Retrieved May 22, 2002 from http://www.ericec.org/osep-sp.html

McLaughlin, M. F., & Nolet, V. (2004). *What every principal needs to know about special education.* Thousand Oaks, CA: Corwin Press.

National Association of Elementary School Principals & ILIAD Project. (2001). *Implementing IDEA: A guide for principals.* Arlington, VA: Council for Exceptional Children and the National Association of Elementary School Principals. Retrieved March 8, 2004 from http://www.ideapractices.org/resources/files/implement.pdf

WEB SITES

The Federal Resource Center for Special Education (FRC)

http://www.dssc.org/frc/oseptad.htm

The FRC supports a nationwide technical assistance network for parents, school districts, and states in special education and disability research.

National Association of State Directors of Special Education (NASDSE)

http://www.nasdse.org

NASDSE provides support to all states and territories in the delivery of quality education to children and youth with disabilities through training, technical assistance, research, policy development, and the development and modeling of powerful collaborative relationships with other organizations and all constituencies.

National Center on Educational Outcomes (NCEO)

http://www.education.umn.edu/nceo/overview/overview.html

The NCEO provides national leadership in designing and building educational assessments and accountability systems that monitor educational results for students with disabilities and students with limited English proficiency. The site includes information on testing accommodations, alternative assessments, grading, and graduation policies.

National Dissemination Center for Children with Disabilities (NICHCY)

http://www.nichcy.org/ideapubs.asp

This Web site provides a wealth of practical information in an easily readable format for administrators, teachers, families, and students about disabilities in children and youth, programs and services for children and youth with disabilities, the Individuals with Disabilities Education Act, No Child Left Behind Act, and effective practices for children with disabilities.

Designing Reasonable Work Assignments

7

Does the job, with all it entails, make sense? Is it feasible? Is it one that well trained, interested, special education professionals can manage in order to accomplish their main objective—enhancing students' academic, social, and vocational competence?

(Gersten et al., 2001, p. 551)

S pecial educators often leave because of problems and frustrations with their work assignments. As Chapter 2 indicates, special educators report concerns about high caseloads, lack of time for their work, excessive paperwork and meetings, and issues in collaborating with general education teachers. These concerns keep teachers from doing their primary work—helping students with disabilities meet their goals.

Teachers need to feel that they reach their students, and their career decisions are tied closely to whether they feel they do (Johnson & Birkeland, 2003a). Structuring special educators' assignments so that they can focus on teaching-related activities needs to be a focus of both school and district leaders.

SCENARIO: "I WANTED TO TEACH KIDS"

Tamara, a former special educator, was interviewed soon after she left her job. After three "miserable" years on the job she accepted a job as a manager at a new Target store that opened in the area. She said, "At least I get paid for my overtime." In discussing her job, she stated, "Most of us entered the [special education] field because we wanted to teach kids, but these activities take a backseat to the paperwork and meetings and all of the legal stuff that we have to do." Tamara also said that "the director [of special education] never asked about my kids; it was 'Did you get that form signed?' 'Did you get this IEP done?' or 'When will some meeting take place?'" Tamara felt her work with students was always on the "backburner." She shared that supervisors rarely asked about her students, what resources she might need to teach them, and how they could support her efforts. Her nonteaching responsibilities were a complicating factor. She stated, "If they [general education teachers] see me doing paperwork or if I'm testing or in meetings they wonder why I'm not working with students. . . . I wanted to teach kids, but that is something I haven't been able to do very much."

CHAPTER OVERVIEW

Tamara's concerns aren't unique. Similar concerns have been documented in a range of special education attrition, stress, and burnout studies (Billingsley, 2004; Kaff, 2004). Conversely, when teachers' roles are wellstructured with adequate time to plan instruction and complete paperwork, they are more likely to stay (Westling & Whitten, 1996).

This chapter provides recommendations for creating work assignments that allow teachers to use their expertise and accomplish their goals. Specifically, this chapter considers:

- Four types of role problems in special education, and
- Strategies for designing reasonable assignments for special educators.

Designing reasonable role assignments requires attention to both *teacher roles* and the *structural* aspects of teachers' work assignments. *Teacher roles* refer to those responsibilities, activities, and tasks that teachers are expected to perform in their work. *Structural aspects* of teachers' work assignments influence what they are able to do (e.g., adequate physical space, availability of materials, and assistance with scheduling).

FOUR TYPES OF ROLE PROBLEMS

Four types of role problems are highlighted in Figure 7.1. Although most special educators will experience these problems at some time, teachers who report chronic problems are more likely to experience stress and role

Role Problems	Definition	Examples	Ways to Help
Role ambiguity	The lack of necessary role information	• Not knowing how to coteach • Lack of clear role expectations • Not knowing how to adjust and change roles in various settings • Lack of understanding about the special educators' role	• Develop role descriptions • Outline goals, procedures, and responsibilities for coteaching • Provide time for teachers to discuss their respective roles
Role dissonance	Teachers' own role expectations differ from the expectations of others	• Being treated as a paraprofessional rather than a teacher • Being unable to use what they know about effective instructional practices • Having a philosophy that is different from the program in which they work • Disagreeing with others how work should be done	• Clarify roles so that each can make the best possible contribution • Ask for the principal's support to solve specific role issues in the school • Help teachers understand that they won't always agree • Keep the student at the center of the conversations
Role conflict	Inconsistent behaviors are expected from the teacher	• Expectations to provide assistance in multiple settings at the same time • Trying to provide help to students and teachers while having to manage excessive bureaucratic responsibilities • Having to neglect regularly scheduled instructional activities to provide help during a crisis	• Schedule the most important activities first • Delegate certain responsibilities to others (e.g., paraprofessionals) • Identify specific role conflict issues and discuss how these can be addressed with administrators and colleagues
Role overload	Having more to do than is reasonable	• Heavy caseloads • Excessive paperwork, testing, and meetings • Demands to collaborate with many people • Feeling pressure because of work	• Limit class size • Computerize IEP process • Allow time for paperwork in weekly schedule • Build collaboration time into schedule • Provide volunteers/aides to assist

Figure 7.1   Special Educators' Role Problems

dissatisfaction, which can result in burnout and attrition (Billingsley, 2004; Gersten et al., 2001). Understanding the nature of these different kinds of role problems is the first step in addressing them.

Special Educators May Be Unclear About Their Roles

Special educators' roles are changing as they work in inclusive classrooms. Rather than "resource teacher," many special educators hold new titles, such as "consulting teacher," "case manager," or "cooperating teacher." These special educators have new and increased responsibilities, and many are not fully prepared for their new roles. Teachers who are unclear about their roles experience *role ambiguity*, or the lack of necessary information for a given position. As one experienced teacher stated as she moved to a position as an inclusion specialist, "I understand we are supposed to kind of like be team teachers in a way. But I'd like to know, what really am I supposed to do?" (Klingner & Vaughn, 2002, p. 25).

Although role descriptions of the resource teacher are better understood, less is known about what inclusion specialists do, and these teachers have fewer precedents to guide them (Klingner & Vaughn, 2002). This leaves teachers with new roles and, in some instances, without preparation or careful consideration of what is needed to perform these roles. Studies of coteaching suggest that teachers and administrators may not understand how to accomplish their work in collaborative settings, or how coteaching will be used to provide specially designed instruction (Weiss & Lloyd, 2002).

Special Educators' Work May Be Misunderstood by Others

Others may not understand the roles and responsibilities of special educators. As the opening scenario with Tamara illustrates, general educators may lack an understanding of special educators' roles. They may expect more from the special education teacher than they can realistically deliver, which can lead to misunderstandings and hard feelings. Another issue is that general educators may fail to understand their own roles in working with special education teachers. Misunderstandings between special and general education teachers can lead to miscommunication and unproductive partnerships.

Special Educators May Be Unable to Accomplish Critical Goals

Special educators are frustrated when they cannot use their expertise in ways that benefit children with disabilities. Special educators, who know how to provide individualized, intensive, research-based interventions, may become discouraged if they find themselves assisting general teachers, acting as "case managers," or trying to provide individualized interventions in classroom settings (Weiss & Lloyd, 2002). When teachers cannot do what they think they should, they experience *role dissonance* (Gersten et al., 2001).

Role conflict occurs when inconsistent behaviors are expected from teachers. Mara, a consulting teacher, was scheduled throughout the day in several different classrooms. The teachers needed her as a coteacher, while the principal expected her to provide crisis interventions for particular students. Mara felt tension because of these differing expectations, but couldn't "find a way out."

Special Educators' Perspectives on Their Workload

You don't only have to test 'em. You have to write up your results. But, before you ever do it, you have to get all these permission forms signed and all the referrals and the request for services—and the paperwork . . . gets worse every year. And then test, write up the results, get all the paperwork ready for the first conference, notify all the other people that have to sit in on that. And then you have your professional conference, and then you have to have another one where the parent comes. And it just goes on and on. And you have paperwork for every one of these conferences.

(From Morvant et al., 1995, pp. 3–14)

I don't know how one teacher is expected to handle the number of students assigned to a caseload. One year I had 50 students with an IEP. Some students were with me all day, others for just 2 or 3 hours. I had to monitor the progress of all of my students whether I saw them a couple of hours a day or for a full day. I had to consult with the regular ed. teacher for all of these 50 kids. It wasn't the lesson planning of daily instruction that was overwhelming; I was responsible for other paperwork for 50 students. My principal felt I shouldn't have a problem with all this paperwork since he assigned me to an assistant for an hour a week. Woo. . . . One hour a week! It didn't matter how hard I tried, I always felt like I was shortchanging the students. If I dealt with the paperwork, I couldn't keep up with the students. If I focused on the students, I couldn't keep up with my paperwork. It was a no-win situation.

SOURCE: Addressing the Revolving Door, 2002, http://iris.peabody.vanderbilt.edu/retention/chalcycle.htm)

Special Educators Struggle With Managing Their Assignments

Special educators experience role overload as they try to juggle complex legal requirements, such as coordinating Individualized Education Programs, assessment reports, and eligibility meetings. Excessive bureaucratic requirements, particularly problems with paperwork, are widely documented in special education (e.g., Billingsley, 2004; Kozleski et al., 2000). As one special educator states:

> I find it hard to meet all of the obligations and expectations placed on me. I am responsible for 33 students spread across four grade levels. My students are in thirteen different classrooms. At the same time, I must run a resource classroom for students. They must be able to come to the resource room at a moment's notice. I am responsible for five paraprofessionals and am the facilitator of the schoolwide problem-solving team. To top it off, I have five students that needed to be tested yesterday (Kaff, 2004, pp. 12–13).

Poorly designed work assignments cost the organization, teacher, as well as families and students with disabilities. For special educators, poor work design prevents them from accomplishing critical goals, which can result in stress, burnout, and attrition. Those frustrated special educators who do stay may lower their expectations for students and themselves. When this happens, students with disabilities lose critical opportunities to learn.

DESIGNING REASONABLE ASSIGNMENTS FOR SPECIAL EDUCATION TEACHERS

Improving teachers' work assignments must begin with an understanding of what special education is designed to do and the specific expectations for special education teachers in the school. Careful role design provides special educators with a clear sense of purpose, and if work conditions are supportive, allows teachers to direct their energy toward valued goals.

Special educators' assignments should be structured so their primary role focuses on supporting students' learning. This means that special educators should be able to devote most of their time to helping students learn or engaging in supports that are directed on their behalf, such as supervising paraprofessionals and collaborating with general education teachers.

What Role Descriptions Can Accomplish

The role problems described in the previous section are due at least in part to poor role design. Many special educators and paraprofessionals operate without job descriptions, leaving them to figure out their roles. Key responsibilities may be misunderstood by others in the school or overlooked by special educators who have minimal or inadequate preparation. Carefully developed role descriptions can help all who work with students with disabilities to better understand their respective roles.

Clarify the Roles of Teachers and Support Personnel

Taking the time to create role descriptions can help teachers, support personnel, and paraprofessionals:

- See the big picture,
- Clarify major job expectations,
- Identify priorities,
- Structure their time,
- Identify areas requiring professional development,
- Identify job tasks that might be shared or delegated, and
- Evaluate their efforts.

Help General Educators Understand Special Educators' Roles

Other school staff may also fail to understand special educators' roles. This often leads to misunderstandings when special educators are released from classes to collaborate with others or when unstated expectations are not fulfilled. For example, Ella Rodriquez, a general education teacher, complained to the principal that Janet, her coteacher, was spending too much time in meetings outside the classroom. Janet did not have an understanding of the range of Ella's responsibilities. Over time, Janet's resentment negatively affected their relationship.

Discussing job descriptions will help communicate:

- The nature and scope of the special educators' roles and activities,
- Differences between varied special educators' roles (e.g., resource teacher, consulting teacher), and
- How special and general educators will work together.

Clarify Collaborative and Coteaching Roles

Special and general educators, as well as paraprofessionals, must clarify how they will work together and describe their respective roles and responsibilities. Principals should not assume that special educators have had significant training in collaborative practices or have a clear understanding of how to work together. Many new special education teachers have not received preservice preparation in collaboration and a third of practicing teachers have not had any recent professional development in collaboration (Local Administrator's Role in Promoting Teacher Quality, 2002). Here, Dr. Lynne Cook provides a perspective on what principals can do to improve collaborative practices in their schools.

The Principal's Role in Facilitating Collaboration: An Interview With Dr. Lynne Cook*

1. What do principals need to know about collaboration?

Successful principals already know a great deal about collaboration. Much of administrative preparation and current literature stresses the importance of fostering collaboration, building teams, and promoting collaborative problem solving. In fact, these skills, or some variation of them, are generally identified as key leadership skills. Establishing a collaborative culture is instrumental in promoting school improvement and student achievement. Fostering collaboration among teachers as well as among teachers and other members of the school community, including parents, is recognized as an important factor in school success.

In terms of serving students, especially those with special needs, collaboration is often a key element in the success of specialized service delivery. When teachers consult with one another about students' unique learning needs or when they plan or teach collaboratively to address those needs, they are often more likely to be able to design and implement targeted interventions and accommodations for students.

Another benefit of collaboration is that it can improve the morale of teachers and reduce their sense of isolation. Teachers who collaborate recognize that they have colleagues on whom they can call for needed assistance and resources. Perhaps one of the greatest benefits is that collaboration is fun! Teachers describe collaborations with others as among the most productive and fun times during their teaching experience.

2. What can principals do to facilitate collaboration between general and special educators?

At the end of the day, the principal may have the most critical role in facilitating collaboration. Much staff development is offered for teachers to learn collaborative skills, but it is of questionable value if schools are not structured to encourage and nurture teacher collaboration. The principal is the individual whose leadership and example makes clear the value of these relationships as well as ensures that teachers have needed time and support to implement collaborative programs and services.

A strong message is conveyed when principals model collaboration and work to ensure that teachers have shared goals, parity—especially in problem solving and decision making—joint responsibility, and accountability. Principals who respect teachers' knowledge and expertise and regularly engage them in decision making about key school issues help to establish a collaborative culture.

One of the more critical supports principals can offer is to arrange for sufficient professional development opportunities for general and special educators to develop communication and collaboration skills. Ideally, principals will participate with teachers in relevant professional development activities. This action goes a long way toward demonstrating that administrators value general and special educator collaboration and that they take seriously their responsibilities for the logistical and administrative supports for programs that entail collaboration.

3. You indicated that professional development is important. What specific topics and skills should be the focus of such training?

Any potential collaborator needs foundational knowledge that includes the understanding of students' needs and the different collaborative structures that might be used to address them. Developing the necessary communication and problem-solving skills is essential. The fundamental interaction process for collaborative work is problem solving. The most straightforward approach is one in which colleagues jointly identify a problem, generate alternative solutions, evaluate potential solutions, and then implement and evaluate the solutions. This is what good teachers do hundreds of times each day: They constantly, and probably automatically, follow these steps in addressing innumerable problems. Then why would they need training to develop and refine this skill? It sounds simple enough, but I've seen time and time again that teachers need significant practice to follow these same steps *with another person.* The problem solving they have been doing automatically and often without directing explicit attention to the process becomes much more challenging when they do it with others. Collaborative problem solving requires participants to slow down. They need to ensure that they understand the problem and the process in the same way and they need to have a shared understanding of their agreed upon solution. Professional development in these and related areas greatly increases the likelihood that collaboration will be successful.

4. What are some specific strategies for creating opportunities for collaboration to occur?

Obviously working collaboratively requires more time for communication and planning. These are a few of the options principals and teachers have found to make the best use of the time available. Some of these must be used infrequently and all should be consistent with good educational practice: (a) designate some of the time set aside for school, grade level, or staff development meetings as collaboration time; (b) create "banked time" by using scheduled early arrival or dismissal time; (c) have other adults such as substitutes, principals, or counselors occasionally help "cover" classes; (d) secure funds for substitutes or find volunteer substitutes; (e) treat collaboration as a responsibility equivalent to committee assignments, lunch or bus duty and use time usually devoted to those activities for collaboration; and (f) use an instructionally relevant presentation or videotape supervised by a limited number of staff while others are released to collaborate. These are but a few of the strategies used in schools.

There are two other considerations that are less frequently addressed. First, the scheduling of instructional periods and classes at both elementary and secondary levels generally influences availability of time for collaborative planning and collaborative service delivery such as coteaching. It may sound blasphemous, but there are real advantages to scheduling instructional periods/classes for students with IEPs first and then building the remainder of the school schedule around that. This allows for far more effective scheduling of teachers' time while maximizing the instructional benefits for students. A related scheduling option is to consider block scheduling, which allows greater flexibility for teacher collaboration. The second sometimes overlooked consideration is explicit skill development for teachers relative to using shared planning time effectively. Few teachers have been prepared with these skills.

> Principals and staff developers can assist teachers to establish ground rules to protect their meeting time, create and follow agendas, keep records, and facilitate meetings.

---

*Dr. Lynne Cook is a professor in the Department of Special Education, California State University, Northridge. She is coauthor of a collaboration text: Friend, M., & Cook, L. (2003). *Interactions: Collaboration Skills for School Professionals* (4th Ed.). Boston: Allyn and Bacon.

Clarify Paraprofessionals' Job Descriptions

Paraprofessionals are increasingly involved in the education of students with disabilities and are usually supervised by special education teachers. Skilled paraprofessionals are a tremendous support to special and general educators and students with disabilities. Special educators need to be involved in hiring the best possible paraprofessionals.

Paraprofessional Requirements Under NCLB

NCLB requires that newly hired paraprofessionals must have met one of the following requirements by January 2, 2002. Those hired after this date have a deadline of January 8, 2006, to complete the requirements. Paraprofessionals must have:

- Completed at least 2 years of study at an institution of higher education, or
- Obtained an associate's or higher degree, or
- Met a rigorous standard of quality and able to demonstrate through a formal state or local academic assessment, knowledge of and the ability to assist in instructing, reading, writing, and mathematics or in readiness activities for reading, writing, or mathematics (NCLB Act of 2001 [Sec.11199c (I)]).

Special educators are usually responsible for orienting and training paraprofessionals, however, they usually have not had any preparation for this role. Further, many paraprofessionals do not have job descriptions to guide their practice, although they are expected to perform a wide range of roles. Paraprofessionals can't do their job well if they don't have a complete understanding of what their work involves. Role descriptions can also be used to identify areas in which paraprofessionals may need training. An example of a job description for paraprofessionals is included in Figure 7.2 (Trautman, 2004).

Resources for Working With Paraeducators

Selected Readings:

Giangreco, M., & Doyle, M. (2002). Students with disabilities and paraprofessional supports. *Focus on Exceptional Children, 34*(7), 1–12.

The role of paraprofessionals in special education. (2000). Rockville, MD: Westat. [Available at www.spense.org.]

Trautman, M. L. (2004). Preparing and managing paraprofessionals. *Intervention in School and Clinic, 39*(3), 131–138.

Selected Web Sites:

Council for Exceptional Children

http://www.cec.sped.org/ps/paraks.html

National Clearinghouse for the Professions in Special Education

http://www.specialedcareers.org/educator_resources/para_resources.html

National Resource Center for Paraprofessionals

http://www.nrcpara.org

U.S. Department of Education on Paraprofessionals and NCLB

http://www.ed.gov/admins/tchrqual/qual/paraprofessional.html?exp=0

How to Develop Role Descriptions

Role descriptions should be developed for each special education position. For example, if both a resource teacher and a consulting teacher work in a school, role descriptions need to reflect their unique responsibilities in the school.

The paraeducator knows and practices good professional ethics by

    a. Keeping information that pertains to school, personnel, students, and parents or guardians confidential; directing communication that concerns the student's program to the child's classroom or IEP manager.
    b. Going directly to his or her supervising teacher, should concerns arise.
    c. Teaming with all school and itinerant staff.

The paraeducator performs the following daily tasks to the best of his or her ability.

    a. Follows programs as written by the teacher.
    b. Reinforces appropriate student behavior as modeled by the teacher and records accurate data when necessary.
    c. Assists teachers in carrying out toileting and feeding programs.
    d. Assists school specialists in physical education, music, and art classes.
    e. Assists the occupational, physical, vision, and speech therapists or other itinerant staff as needed.
    f. Supervises all students in a positive manner.
    g. Responds to emergency situations calmly and appropriately.

The paraeducator and teacher establish a collaborative relationship, with the teacher holding responsibility for the student's program. The paraeducator

    a. Shows a positive attitude toward self-improvement.
    b. Contributes to meetings with the teacher by sharing ideas and observations of students.
    c. Asks clarifying questions when necessary.
    d. Models the teaching and behavior management techniques demonstrated by the teacher.
    e. Takes initiative to carry out responsibilities of supervision.

The paraeducator follows the listed school philosophies, guidelines, and procedures.

    a. Notifies the supervising teacher if an absence is scheduled in advance.
    b. Prepares a substitute folder.
    c. Arranges breaks and lunch with teacher.
    d. Arrives promptly and follows the daily schedule.
    e. Manages time efficiently during school hours.
    f. Dresses appropriately.
    g. Attends the scheduled paraeducator meetings.

The paraeducator demonstrates the understanding that all students enrolled at ____ school have individual and special learning needs. He or she

    a. Respects the right of the student to a least restrictive environment.
    b. Provides an environment that protects the student's human dignity.
    c. Displays a positive attitude when working with students.
    d. Encourages student independence.
    e. Models age-appropriate behavior.

The paraeducator shares responsibilities for housekeeping and clerical duties.

    a. Prepares the classroom before students arrive.
    b. Prepares or gathers materials students may need during the day.
    c. Cleans classrooms as needed throughout the day.
    d. Follows schedules for filling and collecting spray bottles, arranging communication systems, etc.
    e. Prepares materials as directed by teacher.
    f. Contributes to team efforts to keep work areas neat.

Goal 1: To provide support to the student during academic, social, vocational, and leisure activities.

Goal 2: To enable students to become independent in their daily routines.

Goal 3: To provide support to the classroom teachers of our students.

Figure 7.2   Roles and Responsibilities of Paraeducators

SOURCE: Trautman, M. L. (2004). Preparing and managing paraprofessionals. *Intervention in the School and Clinic, 39*(3), 131–138. By PRO-ED, Inc. Adapted with permission.

Special Education Teaching and Progress Monitoring:

- Implements curriculum and educational programs for all eighth grade students with learning disabilities and emotional disorders in accordance with the IEP.
- Monitors performance of students on LD/ED roster in eighth grade classes.
- Provides individualized assistance in a resource class for students with individualized reading and writing IEP goals (two periods daily).
- Maintains ongoing records of student progress toward goals and communicates progress to parents every six weeks.

Collaboration:

- Collaborates with general education teachers in the development of IEPs.
- Meets with grade level team on a weekly basis.
- Assists classroom teachers with student problems and issues.
- Provides general educators with assistance with curricular modifications, instructional adaptations, and assessment accommodations.
- Assists with developing positive behavioral support plans and behavior contracts.
- Supervises and plans with three paraprofessionals.
- Encourages parental involvement in program and communicates progress as necessary (but no less than every three weeks).

Coteaches for two periods daily, including the following activities:

- Adapts lesson goals, presentations, and materials.
- Provides small-group and individualized instruction.
- Reteaches content on specific skills.
- Assists in organization, management, and class discipline.
- Monitors student progress in class and assiss with testing modifications.

Testing, Record Keeping, and Compliance:

- Monitors screening, IEP, and reevaluations for all eight grade students.
- Makes new referrals to the testing coordinator.
- Maintains legal records and documents for all students on the eighth grade roster.
- Shares key legal information with new general educators and paraprofessionals (e.g., confidentiality, IEP requirements, legal principles of IDEA).

Figure 7.3   Role Description for a Special Education Teacher of Students With Learning Disabilities and Emotional Disorders 2004–2005 School Year (Grade 8)

Begin With an Existing Description

Begin with an existing description or make a list of current responsibilities. Consider the key roles and the range of responsibilities that special education teachers should address (e.g., instruction, parents, collaboration, record keeping). Another way of drafting a description is to consider descriptions used in other schools or use the descriptions in Figures 7.2 and 7.3. Revise the list by eliminating those that do not apply and add others that are important.

Encourage Broad Levels of Input

Ideally, both school leaders and faculty will have input concerning how students with disabilities will be served in the school and the respective roles of both special and general educators in their education. These discussions can also be used to develop specific processes for collaborative relationships. For example, in coteaching situations, teachers can develop a process that includes:

- A discussion of student goals,
- What adaptations are required in the curriculum to meet the goals,
- What additional specialized instruction is needed,
- How assessments will be completed, and
- Who is responsible for each of the tasks.

Consider the Council for Exceptional Children's Code of Ethics

The Council for Exceptional Children (CEC) has a code of ethics for members of the special education profession. Reviewing the Code of Ethics as the job role is developed will help educators consider a full range of responsibilities. The Code of Ethics for educators of students with disabilities includes eight major areas:

- Commitment to developing the highest educational and quality of life potential for individuals with disabilities;
- Promoting and maintaining a high level of competence and integrity in professional practices;
- Engaging in professional activities that benefit individuals with disabilities, their families, colleagues, and others;
- Exercising objective professional judgment in the practice of their work;
- Striving to advance their knowledge and skills in educating students with disabilities;
- Working within the standards and policies of their profession; and
- Upholding and improving the laws, regulations, and policies governing the provision of special education and related services.

Detailed responsibilities under each of these areas are available on the CEC Web site: http://www.cec.sped.org

Determine Whether the Description Is Complete and Reasonable

Role descriptions should be evaluated periodically, considering whether the role description is complete, sufficiently detailed, and clear. Role descriptions must be modified as needs change. In evaluating role descriptions it is helpful to ask several questions:

- Is the role description consistent with what special education programs are designed to accomplish?
- Is it designed so that special educators can meet their obligations to students with disabilities?
- Is the role description complete? Are any key roles missing?
- Is it reasonable? Can the special educator realistically carry out this role?
- What do special and general educators think about the role as described?
- What difficulties might be encountered given the present role description?
- How might these be solved?

Reduce Role Overload

After teacher roles have been clarified and discussed among all involved, reducing role overload is one of the most important ways to help teachers focus on their central role of supporting students' learning. Many leaders assume that little can be done about the paperwork and meetings in special education. However, this is not the case. For example, North Carolina passed a paperwork reduction bill that gives teachers the right to refuse requests for data that they have already provided. Others have negotiated for standardized IEP forms, release time, and additional compensation (Holcomb, Admundson, & Ralabate, 2002).

District administrators who are serious about reducing nonteaching duties can find solutions to at least reduce the burden on teachers. Sometimes states and districts actually have requirements that are not mandated by IDEA. Do an audit of your processes and forms. Ask teachers to work with you to identify areas of concern and suggestions.

Reduce the Number of Students on Caseloads

Special educators who leave often identify caseload issues as a reason. Caseload issues are related not just to the number of students served, but the diversity of caseloads. Special educators who plan to leave their positions as soon as possible were more likely to teach students with four or more primary disabilities (Carlson & Billingsley, 2001).

Caseloads in special education have been growing and are approaching those of general education (McLeskey et al., 2004). Teachers with high caseloads not only have less opportunity to individualize instruction, they also have increased paperwork and additional teachers with whom they must collaborate.

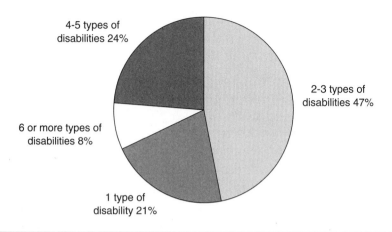

Figure 7.4 Numbers of Different Disabilities on Special Educators' Caseloads
SOURCE: Carlson et al., 2002. Used with permission.

Unfortunately, several states do not limit caseloads. Local leaders should consider contacting the state education agency to address caseload issues and protect special education teachers from unreasonable loads. If reducing the caseload is not possible, then try to provide some relief by offering clerical assistance or release time to offset the load.

Eliminate or Delegate Nonteaching Tasks

How can noninstructional tasks be minimized or organized so that special educators are able to focus on their primary teaching-related responsibilities? This requires answering the following questions:

- What are the nonteaching tasks for which the special educator currently has responsibility?
- Are all of these tasks essential?
- If not, which can be eliminated?
- Can any of the tasks be revised to take less time?
- Can any of these tasks (or a portion of these tasks) be delegated? If not, can a particular time be set aside for this task?

For example, although special educators may need to assist with some aspects of referral and eligibility for special education, trained clerical workers can keep track of whether eligibility components have been completed, mail forms, and schedule meetings.

Streamline Paperwork Requirements

Special educators complain that excessive time is spent on paperwork. Over half of elementary and secondary special education teachers report that routine duties and paperwork greatly interfere with their job of teaching. Excessive paperwork is also related to feelings of reduced manage-ability and greater intent to leave teaching (Paperwork in Special Education, 2002). Consider those aspects of paperwork that can be modified, delegated to clerical staff, or eliminated as noted in the following examples:

- Ensure all paperwork is necessary.
- Streamline paperwork requirements.
- Eliminate redundant requests for class roles and reports.
- Ensure that directions for completing paperwork requirements and timelines are clear.
- Eliminate the need for paper by using electronic forms and make student databases available to teachers at all times.
- Ask special educators who are highly organized to share their systems for managing their paperwork and time.
- Ask special educators for suggestions on changing district forms to make reporting requirements more efficient.
- Set a goal for the amount of average weekly time that teachers must spend weekly on nonteaching-related paperwork (e.g., three hours or less).
- Pay paraprofessionals or clerical assistants for an additional hour each day to assist teachers with paperwork and record keeping.

Are You Doing Unnecessary Work?

- "Does your school hold too many IEP meetings? The minimum required for a student is one a year. You don't need to hold an IEP meeting unless you're changing the student's placement, the program goals, or the services that are provided—or unless the school district or parents request a meeting."
- "Some teachers believe they have to write a goal for every single class the student is taking. . . . You only have to write goals for need areas. If a student's difficulties are only in reading, you don't need to write math goals."
- "Some teachers are under the impression that every IEP requires a behavioral component. This is true only if the student's behavior impedes his or her learning and/or the learning of other students."

SOURCE: Holcomb, S., Admundson, E., & Ralabate, P. (2002). *The New IDEA Survival Guide.* Retrieved July 18, 2004 from http://home.nea.org/books.

Evaluate the IEP Process

Under recent deliberations in the reauthorization of IDEA, the IEP was considered a major contributor to the paperwork problem in special education. However, individual planning with the involvement of parents and teachers has always been a major principle of IDEA. Keeping the IEP process and making it work well is important to ensuring that students with disabilities receive programs based on their needs. To improve the district IEP process:

- Ask teachers and parents what is working well and what needs to be revised;
- Streamline the IEP process and limit the document to several pages;
- Use software programs that reduce the time needed to score tests and write IEPs;
- Link general education curriculum goals to IEP software programs;
- Ensure that teachers have the knowledge and skills to efficiently implement the IEP process; and
- Ensure that teachers have the needed materials for the process.

**Cut Paperwork and Save Money
With Automated IEP Solutions**

Many automated IEP products offer solutions to the special education paperwork burden. Web-based solutions streamline the sharing of information throughout the district and track Medicaid dollars to keep money coming back to the district. Typical solutions offer districts the choice to install and host the IEP system themselves or have the vendor host it. Costs associated with IEP software usually include an initial license fee, setup fees, training fees, an annual support fee, and associated IT hardware costs.

Given the strength of many automated IEP solutions today, districts have few reasons to not automate their IEP process. When evaluating software solutions, administrators should look for solutions that are fairly priced, flexible, and aligned with the district's IT infrastructure. Teachers should be able to learn the software in a day or two, and the solution should be Webbased to facilitate real-time information sharing and to minimize IT infrastructure requirements.

One solution, IEP.Online was recently recognized in the June issue of *District Administration* magazine as a Top 100 product.

> Other solutions are available, but it is important to do your homework. With the right technology solutions, schools can reduce paperwork, go online, and save time and money!

SOURCE: *CEC Today*, Vol. 10, No. 4, November–December 2003. Reprinted with permission of the Council for Exceptional Children.

Provide Structural Supports

Structural supports are those physical and organizational aspects of work needed for teachers to accomplish their goals. Teachers need adequate physical facilities to do their work and conduct assessments. They also need teaching materials, supplies, and assistive technology to use in their work with students. Teachers and students must carefully coordinate their schedules so that instruction can occur. Helping teachers with specific supports—such as providing needed materials, space, and resources—has a positive effect on their satisfaction and commitment (Billingsley, 2004).

Supply Adequate Materials

Special educators often report that they have inadequate materials. Special educators who lack adequate instructional materials are forced to develop their own materials, or copy existing materials. Special educators, like general educators, need to have:

- Adequate materials for their teaching,
- Discretionary funds to purchase what they need,
- Teachers' manuals and support materials, and
- Assistive technology for their students.

Consider Supports for Scheduling

Special educators who work in resource and consulting teacher positions often find scheduling students to be a major issue. Take time to identify what is creating the scheduling problem. Although there are few absolutes about scheduling, consider strategies such as:

- Giving special education teachers input into the master schedule,
- Assigning special educators to a particular grade or grades to allow the teacher to be part of a team, and
- Allowing teachers to hand schedule their students.

TIPS FOR LEADERS

Ask Teachers What They Need

Teachers appreciate being asked about their work and what they need to accomplish their goals. School and district leaders who understand special educators' needs will be better able to allocate resources to important needs.

Include Teachers in Budget Decisions

Teachers who are involved in budget decisions have input into how funds are spent and also develop an appreciation for district and school constraints.

Support Teachers in Identifying Solutions to Their Problems

Teachers should be involved in both assessing problems and seeking solutions to problems. For example, if using software programs to reduce the paperwork in special education is considered, teachers need to be involved in evaluating and selecting such programs.

Give Teachers Time to Get Used to Changing Roles

Special educators react differently to their changing roles. Some see role changes as necessary to achieve a unified system of education that serves all students. Others feel threatened by the changes because they have been asked to take on new roles, have less control over their work, or disagree with new service-delivery models. Listen to their concerns—they likely have valid points that need to be addressed.

Remain Open—Avoid Becoming Defensive About Teacher Complaints

Listen to teachers' complaints. Why are they complaining? Do they have the time, resources, and physical space needed for their work? If not, they are only asking for what they need to do their work well. Even if you can't help solve the problem, you can listen. I often worried more about the teachers I supervised who never asked for anything.

SUMMARY

- Special educators who have unclear roles, conflicting expectations, and excessive bureaucratic responsibilities often experience frustration, stress, and burnout.

- Special educators' work assignments should be structured to allow them to focus on their students' needs.
- Teachers who have well-designed roles and structural supports are able to divide their time reasonably among their responsibilities.
- Principals can help special educators by learning about how their assignments are structured, working to clarify their roles, communicating about their roles with general educators, and assuring the structural supports necessary for their work.

SELECTED READINGS

CEC Code of Ethics and Standards of Practice http://www.cec.sped.org/ps/code.html

Friend, M., & Cooke, L. (2003). *Interactions: Collaboration skills for school professionals (4th Ed.)*. Boston: Allyn & Bacon.

Holcomb, S., Admundson, E., & Ralabate, P. (2002). *The new IDEA survival guide*. National Education Association (http://home.nea.org/books).

Studies of Personnel Needs in Special Education (SPeNSE). (2002). *Paperwork in special education*. Retrieved February 6, 2003 from http://ferdig.coe.ufl.edu/spense/Paperwork.doc

WEB SITES

IEP Online

http://www.ieponline.net/

IEP.Online and MED.Online are products designed to manage student child study, eligibility, IEP processing, 504 documentation, caseload management, and Medicaid reimbursement.

Individualized Classroom Accountability Network (ICAN)

https://ican.doe.state.in.us/

ICAN provides a time-saving electronic database that can be used to assist with a range of tasks (e.g., develop IEPs, develop lesson plans, track student progress).

Promoting Wellness by Reducing Stress **8**

To be effective, educators must give themselves permission to have their own needs met.

(Luckner, 1996, p. 27)

Although special education teaching can be a very stressful job, we don't take the stress that educators experience seriously. Unfortunately, the consequences of stressful work environments are high for both teachers and the organizations for which they work. Teachers who experience high levels of prolonged stress are at a greater risk for depression, burnout, and illness. On an organizational level, work-related stress contributes to low morale, low work performance, burnout, withdrawal, absenteeism, and attrition (Wisniewski & Gargiulo, 1997; Zabel & Zabel, 2001). Consider these findings:

- Stress is a major predictor of special education attrition (Miller et al., 1999),
- 39% of teachers who transferred from special to general education teaching identified "burnout" from teaching in special education as a primary reason (Billingsley & Cross, 1991),
- Teachers reporting higher levels of stress are more likely to want to leave (Gersten et al., 2001), and
- Special educators experience steady increases in emotional exhaustion over the first five years of teaching (Frank & McKenzie, 1993).

SCENARIO: "WHERE'S THE JOY?"

Caleb, an idealistic and committed special educator, began teaching with high expectations. He gave 110% to his new job. It wasn't unusual to see Caleb at school after hours and on the weekends—he was willing to put in whatever time was necessary to accomplish his goals. Although his first years of teaching went well, Caleb's joy began to fade with the increasing frustrations he felt in his work. Although the lack of time to collaborate with general educators was always a problem, his irritation with his colleagues grew stronger over time. He didn't understand why they didn't want to do more to help students with disabilities in their classes. Caleb's colleagues retorted that he was, after all, the special educator. Caleb began to take his colleagues' objections personally and his resentment continued to build. The principal listened to his concerns but reminded Caleb that the other teachers had many students to consider. Caleb wondered why he even bothered trying since "the principal doesn't get it and the teachers won't budge." Over time, the workload, the lack of cooperation from his colleagues, and the limited resources overwhelmed Caleb; he became cynical and withdrew. During his exit interview, Caleb summed up his reason for leaving: "I just couldn't do what I needed to do. . . . I just don't have the energy anymore."

CHAPTER OVERVIEW

The psychological needs of teachers are often ignored. However, principals and district leaders who understand stress and burnout are better able to promote wellness in the workplace. Specifically, this chapter addresses:

- Symptoms of teacher stress and burnout,
- Contributors to stress and burnout,
- Assessing stress and burnout, and
- Strategies to reduce stress and promote wellness.

SYMPTOMS OF TEACHER STRESS AND BURNOUT

Stressors are experiences that individuals interpret as taxing or troublesome (Wisniewski & Gargiulo, 1997). Symptoms of stress may be emotional, behavioral, and physical. Emotional and behavior symptoms include frustration, anxiety, irritability, anger, guilt, worry, tension, or depression. Physical symptoms include tight muscles, headaches, fatigue, nervous tics, and high blood pressure (Howatt, 2001).

STRESS

S = stuck in a thought

T = tolerance for situation gone

R = real to me

E = ending to something or threatening a want

S = sick feeling in body

S = self-esteem damaged

SOURCE: Howatt, 2001.

Burnout results when teachers are no longer able to cope with work-related stress. Burnout is about "inconsequentiality," wherein teachers view that the work is endless, their endeavors are ineffective, and there is little recognition or appreciation for their efforts (Farber, 2000).

Changes in attitude often signal burnout. These teachers may be negative, have fewer goals, show less idealism, become inflexible, or show greater self-interest (Farber, 2000; Hughes, 2001). Three major features characterize burnout (Maslach, Jackson, & Leiter, 1996):

1. *Emotional exhaustion:* the feeling that one has little to give others emotionally or psychologically;

2. *Depersonalization:* detachment from others; and

3. *Reduced professional accomplishment:* feelings of ineffectiveness in their professional responsibilities.

Burnout is the loss of commitment (LeCompte & Dworkin, 1991). Many teachers experiencing burnout want to quit their jobs. Although some of these teachers leave, others stay, but have less energy for new learning, supporting others, and teaching their students (Billingsley, 2004).

CONTRIBUTORS TO STRESS AND BURNOUT

This section outlines major stressors experienced by special education teachers and addresses the role of teacher perceptions and expectations.

Major Stressors Experienced by Special Educators

The stressors special educators report and special educators' reasons for leaving teaching overlap. Figure 8.1 provides a list of major stressors

Work Assignment Problems

Difficulty meeting students' needs
Inappropriate student placements
Problems with student discipline and motivation
Heavy caseloads, workloads, and time pressures
Conflicting or unclear expectations
Legal pressures and concerns
Accountability and testing demands

Inadequate Support

Absence of leadership support for special education
Minimal support for collaboration
Few instructional and technological resources
Inadequate feedback about teaching
Lack of professional development opportunities
Minimal help from leaders with issues and problems
Lack of influence in decision making
Lack of parent support

Relationship Concerns

Feelings of isolation
Stressful interactions with others (e.g., students, parents, teachers, administrators)
Conflicts with general educators over inclusion

Lack of Rewards

Lack of student progress
Lack of professional satisfaction
Minimal appreciation or recognition for work

Figure 8.1   Special Education Teacher Stressors

SOURCE: Kozleski et al., 2000; Wisniewski & Gargiulo, 1997.

identified in special education studies. High caseloads, role conflict, excessive paperwork and meetings, isolation, and problems in collaboration are common themes in both stress and attrition studies (compare with Figure 2.1). Special educators working primarily as team or consulting teachers are at a greater risk of burnout than teachers who work in resource and self-contained classrooms. Team teachers sometimes work in general education classrooms where they may be unwelcome and their responsibilities include a wider range of services (Embich, 2001).

How Perceptions and Unmet Needs Contribute to Stress

Stress is influenced by teachers' *perceptions* of situations. Teachers may react quite differently to similar situations. Some teachers find small annoyances stressful while others experience resilience in the face of very difficult situations. In particular, highly idealistic teachers like Caleb are more likely to feel stressed because high expectations may not be met in the reality of schools.

Leaders also contribute to the problem of unmet expectations. Leaders who establish expectations, but do not provide the resources or organizational structures to help teachers meet these expectations, unwittingly contribute to teachers' anxiety and stress (Wisniewski & Gargiulo, 1997). Teachers are also likely to feel stressed when their needs are not met. Teachers want to feel competent, connected to others, and have an influence in the decisions that affect them. When teachers, needs consistently go unmet, they experience frustration and stress.

ASSESSING STRESS AND BURNOUT

Given the high costs of stress and burnout to individuals and organizations, leaders need to watch for signs of teacher stress and burnout. Assessment instruments can be used to help leaders and teachers identify specific stressors, so they can intervene before burnout occurs. Teachers who assess their own stress levels will become aware of stress "triggers" and consider how they might be managed.

Selecting Instruments

Although several teacher stress scales exist, principals and district administrators should identify whether the instrument will help them meet their specific purposes for administration. They may want to consult with university faculty or local school employees who have background in test selection, administration, and interpretation (e.g., evaluation and testing specialists, school psychologists).

Examples of Instruments

The Teacher Stress Inventory

The Teacher Stress Inventory (TSI), developed by Fimian (1988), assesses stress on ten different factors (see Resource B to review the complete inventory). The inventory helps identify specific stress-related problems in the school or district. Individuals can also assess their own stress levels and determine how their stress levels compare to norms. The TSI manual and a text version of the stress inventory are available for use without charge from The Teacher Stress Inventory Web site: http://www.instructionaltech.net/tsi/

Maslach Burnout Inventory

The most widely used instrument for assessing burnout is the Maslach Burnout Inventory (Maslach et al., 1996). An educator version is also available. The Maslach assesses three aspects of educator burnout for teachers, aides, and administrators. The inventory is available through Career/LifeSkills Resources, Inc. For more information, see http://www.career-lifeskills.com/products_services/atpr/corpcultdev/cpp-34500.htm

Strategies to Reduce Stress and Promote Wellness

More attention has been focused on describing stress and burnout among special educators than on devising interventions to reduce stress. There are two major approaches to reducing stress and burnout. The first is to modify aspects of the organization, school, and classroom that contribute to stress. Ideally, efforts to change the functioning of the school and assignment should prevent high levels of stress and subsequent burnout (Farber, 2000). The second approach is to help teachers develop awareness about their own stress, recognize what contributes to their stress, and to learn strategies for coping with the everyday strains of school life (Cooley & Yovanoff, 1996; Howatt, 2001). Ideally, both organizational and individual interventions will be considered.

Stress and burnout can affect teachers in different ways. The chart in Figure 8.2 provides an overview of Farber's (2000) discussion of three types of burnout, including "worn-out," "classic," and "underchallenged." Included in Figure 8.2 are both the beliefs and behaviors that are associated with the three types of burnout. Different types of burnout may require different kinds of interventions. For example, although teachers exhibiting the "classic" type of burnout will likely benefit from stress reduction activities, the "underchallenged" teacher will probably benefit less from these activities (Farber, 2000).

Organizational Strategies

Unfortunately, stress and burnout are often viewed as "personal" issues, which minimize the need to address the organizational contributors to stress and burnout. Teachers need safe and caring environments with strong social support networks. The reality is that special educators' work assignments are often poorly designed and they have inadequate supports. Throughout this book, the problems that many special education teachers experience and steps that leaders can take to improve

Type of Burnout	Teacher Beliefs/ Thoughts	Teacher Behaviors	Interventions
"Wear-out" or "Brown-out"	Efforts will not lead to desired results (learned helplessness) Focuses on failures rather than successes Views the future work situation as bleak	Gives up, stops trying to succeed Shows lack of effort or perfunctory work performance	• Help teachers reinvest in their work • Encourage teachers to connect to their reasons for teaching • Facilitate teacher socialization with others who are invested in their work • Encourage teachers to focus on what is going well • Provide technical advice (e.g., find ways of working with problematic situations)
"Classic"	Views problems as a failure of will Believes that greater effort will lead to success Perceives that they are a failure if they are not perfect or unless all of their students succeed	Works increasingly hard when confronting stress Exerts excessive effort on behalf of students Efforts lead to exhaustion	• Encourage teachers to care for self and find a balance between work and other areas of their lives • Provide opportunities to reduce stress • Encourage counseling (may help address the roots of perfectionism)
"Underchallenged"	Experiences work as monotonous or uninteresting Finds little meaning in teaching	Shows boredom or disinterest	• Remind teacher of past and present successes • Help teachers see the need for their work • Challenge the teacher by encouraging new experiences and opportunities (e.g., different assignments, new projects)

Figure 8.2 Types of Teacher Burnout and Suggested Interventions

SOURCE: Adapted from Farber, B.A. (2000). Treatment strategies for different types of teacher burnout. *Psychotherapy in Practice, 56*(5), 675–689.

special educators' work environments are addressed. In particular, strong leadership in special education, responsive teacher induction and mentoring programs, collaborative environments, opportunities for professional development, and well-designed work assignments will do much to reduce the stress that special educators experience (see Chapters 4–7).

Coping Strategies

Even with well-designed work environments, special education teachers need to learn to cope with unexpected problems, crises, and day-to-day hassles and disappointments. This section outlines recommendations to help teachers learn to cope with stress.

Help Teachers Develop an Awareness of Stress

Teachers who begin to feel stress have reached their "personal frustration tolerance threshold" (Howatt, 2001). One misconception about stress is that people know when they are stressed. This is not necessarily the case. Over time, prolonged stress can begin to feel normal. Not all teachers will find the same things stressful. It is helpful for teachers to identify specific situations that trigger stress, including particular times of the day or year, or specific people or habits of others. Posting a stress questionnaire in the teachers' lounge may help teachers consider the extent of their own stress.

Encourage Self-Care

Physical health is important to mental and emotional balance, and teachers are more likely to feel stressed if they are tired and poorly nourished. The four pillars of health include exercise, a healthy diet, adequate rest, and relaxation (Howatt, 2001). Some school districts have policies that encourage good health, such as health screening exams, early release for exercise, and healthy lunches and snacks. Classes in yoga and relaxation can help reduce teacher stress as well.

Help Teachers Establish Realistic Expectations

As stated above, highly committed and idealistic teachers may be particularly vulnerable to burnout. Jean, a dedicated and effective special education teacher, worked after school hours every day and often on the weekend during her first several years of teaching. By the end of the fourth year she felt tired and wondered whether she could keep up. Jean needed to learn to prioritize her goals and learn to let go of unnecessary work.

Help Teachers Develop a Sense of Efficacy

Teachers who have a strong sense of efficacy have confidence in their abilities to teach and know that they have the skills to do their work (Brownell, 1997). Because burnout is about "inconsequentiality" (Farber, 2000), teachers need to learn how to assess whether or not their efforts are making a difference. This is particularly important because NCLB student testing requirements can be discouraging for students with disabilities, their teachers, and parents. These standardized assessments are not always appropriate for students with disabilities, and students' performance on these tests may give students and teachers a sense of failure, even when significant progress is made. Teachers need to be encouraged to use appropriate assessments, such as curriculum-based measurement, which are sensitive to small increments of student change (Greer & Greer, 1992). Professional development activities are also important to helping teachers continue to build their knowledge and skills.

Provide Help With Organizational Strategies

Setting realistic goals, establishing priorities, and developing strong organizational skills are learned behaviors. Teachers need to be clear about their long-range goals, develop a plan to meet them, set short-term goals, and schedule time to address them. After determining goals, teachers need to work to ensure that their daily schedules are consistent with their goals (Luckner, 1996). Stephen Covey's book, *The Seven Habits of Effective People,* is a helpful resource for those who want to try to sort out their priorities and "put first things first." Mentors can also help new teachers establish reasonable work expectations during the first years of teaching. Experienced teachers who have strong organizational skills can also share their strategies with others.

Facilitate Social Support

Supportive colleagues are an important buffer against stress. Teachers who work in school climates that encourage collegiality, problem solving, and emotional support experience less stress. Scheduling social activities, especially those that occur outside of work, allow teachers to interact in more relaxed settings. Voluntary teacher support groups like those described in Figure 8.3 and the "Interventions" box below can help teachers meet personal and professional needs and give teachers time to address concerns. Specific problem-solving strategies and guidelines should be established by the group so that meetings are productive.

Address Conflicts in the School

Conflict is an inevitable part of relationships. Without strategies for handling differences, conflicts with parents, colleagues, administrators, and teachers can escalate into situations that create stress and disrupt interpersonal relationships. Leaders can model "win-win" ways of addressing conflicts (Covey, 1989). Primary considerations in addressing conflicts include:

1. Looking for solutions and avoiding blaming others;

2. Keeping important goals at the center of discussions, such as what is best for students; and

3. Using good communication skills, such as "I" messages to express feelings, needs, and concerns.

Conflict resolution and mediation skills are worthy professional development goals.

Help Teachers Find a Balance of Concern

Many of the special educators are highly empathetic and concerned teachers. Consider Susan, a sensitive and empathetic teacher who showed a high level of dedication toward her students. She visited her students' homes, purchased clothes that they needed, and tried to help with many needs beyond the classroom. Although her dedication was admirable, she "absorbed" many of her students' problems and concerns. Susan "overidentified" with her students, and often took their problems home with her. Although empathy is a desirable characteristic in special educators, overinvolvement leads to problems, such as emotional exhaustion and detachment (Greer & Greer, 1992).

Help Others Learn to Not Take Things Personally

It is easy to take some types of problems personally. For example, when a parent or colleague expresses unhappiness or disapproval, a teacher's first reaction may be to feel attacked and defensive. Tina, an early career teacher, complained about a student's mother who had become verbally abusive to her during a phone call. Over the past year, Tina had worked hard to help the child with significant behavioral issues, and felt "devastated" by the mother's criticisms about her. After discussing the interaction with her principal, Tina learned that the mother also had similar interactions with other teachers and administrators in prior years. It was important for Tina to realize that the mother's anger was not a reflection on the quality of her work with the student.

Programs Designed to Provide Support and Reduce Stress

This section highlights programs designed to support teachers and reduce stress. These programs help teachers with problem solving, developing self-awareness and coping skills, and encouraging colleague support. Leaders interested in reducing teacher stress should consider aspects of these three programs.

School Wellness Programs

District and school policies can be developed to encourage wellness and provide knowledge and information for addressing stress in the workplace. One independent, K–12 school developed a wellness program to improve teacher retention and teachers' mental and physical health. Activities are based on an assessment of teachers' needs. The program included:

1. Readings in the faculty lounge about wellness topics,

2. Daily fresh fruit in the faculty lounge,

3. An on-campus Weight Watchers program,

4. Regularly scheduled yoga classes, and

5. Annual wellness events.

These annual events included workshops on stress management and art therapy and fitness activities requiring group problem solving and cooperation (Davies, Davies, & Heacock, 2003).

Regional Teacher Support Program (TSP

The TSP is a regional program that includes a range of activities designed to support and retain teachers of students with disabilities in Western North Carolina (Westling & Cooper-Duffy, 2003). The program includes varied types of support including collaborative problem solving and mutual teacher support sessions, electronic networking, information and materials search, and on-site consultation (see Figure 8.3).

Teaching Stress Management and Collaborative Skills

The box on pages 168–171 highlights two interventions designed to help teachers develop strategies for coping with stress and to prevent burnout and teacher attrition. Cooley and Yovanoff (1996) designed these interventions to help special educators deal with the stressors in their immediate environment. The first intervention helps teachers learn to manage stress by:

TSP Components	Description
Teacher Support Program (TSP) is designed to support and retain teachers of students with disabilities in Western North Carolina.	
Collaborative Problem Solving/Mutual Teacher Support Sessions	Ten to twelve sessions were provided per semester in four separate sites to help teachers work collaboratively, assist each other with problems, and provide general support. Teachers used notebooks to work in small groups, and used specific problem-solving steps as outlined in the notebook.
Electronic Networking and Communications	Blackboard.com was used to post announcements, host discussions, and encourage communication with others.
Information and Materials Search	A materials and information search service was provided to participants.
Mentoring	Teachers with more experience provide mentoring to their less-experienced counterparts. Mentors also assist during problem-solving sessions and by phone or e-mail.
On-Site/In-Class Consultation	Participants may request assistance from the coordinator, project directors, or member of the project staff. Observations were followed by conferences to discuss concerns.
Teacher Release for Professional Development	Substitute teachers were provided so the participant could participate in professional development activities.
Participant-Designed Workshops	Two staff development sessions are provided each semester with participants identifying and designing the nature of the sessions.

Figure 8.3   Teacher Support Program

SOURCE: Westling, D. L., & Cooper-Duffy, K. (2003). The Western Carolina University Teacher Support Program: A multi-component program to improve and retain special educators. *Teacher Education and Special Education, 26*(2), 154–158.

1. Changing the situation,

2. Changing their response to the situation, and

3. Changing how they think about the situation.

Intervention 2 is a peer dialogue program that helps teachers identify and solve student-related problems.

TIPS FOR LEADERS

Understand Local Stressors Affecting Special Educators

Take time to answer the following questions:

- What are the major problems that special educators are experiencing in your district or school?
- What needs to be changed to reduce these stressors?

Realize That Specific Groups May Be Particularly Susceptible to Stress

Certain groups of special education teachers are more susceptible to stress than others. For example, new teachers are at risk for stress because they are facing many new demands and lack established support systems. Itinerant teachers have the additional load of travel and the stress of managing their work in multiple places. Itinerant teachers also have fewer opportunities to be part of a school support network and may not be included in school events.

Schedule a "Stress Awareness" Session

Becoming aware of what contributes to teachers' stress need not take a great deal of time. For example, in a one-hour session:

- Ask teachers to complete Fimian's stress questionnaire (Resource B) and ask them to identify major stressors;
- Ask what can happen in the school (or district) environment to reduce some of these stressors; and
- Share strategies for coping with stress (Brownell, 1997; Howatt, 2001; Luckner, 1996).

Encourage Teachers to Connect to Their Profession

Special educators usually have only a few other special educators to work with on a regular basis. They may feel alone in their stress, especially if the other teachers around them have different concerns. Encourage special educators to connect to the larger community of special educators in the district and to use their professional organization's network of teachers.

Focus on What Is Meaningful

Teachers sometimes need to revisit why they became special educators. Experienced teachers who remain motivated and excited about their work year after year focus on what they are able to accomplish and take pride in their accomplishments.

Provide Support During Conflicts

Special education teachers who are involved in conflicts with parents or due process hearings often feel high levels of stress associated with these events. Taking time to prepare the teacher for due process hearings is important. Equally important is encouraging the teachers and letting them know that they will be supported in the process.

Focus on the Positive and Use Humor

Leaders can model a positive outlook, avoid criticizing others, and focus on what is going well. Looking for the humor in daily situations keeps things in perspective and makes it easier to cope.

Interventions

Intervention 1: Stress Management-Burnout Prevention Workshops

Many of the stressful aspects of the special education teaching profession are either inherent to the situation or difficult to change. Moreover, the burnout that often results from demanding and stressful working conditions can itself exacerbate difficulties because of its accompanying negative, self-defeating coping behaviors. Coping takes many forms. Approaches to handling stress may be either *direct* (e.g., changing the source of stress) or *indirect* (e.g., changing the way one thinks about or physically responds to the stress to reduce its impact). In addition, coping strategies may be *active* (e.g., taking some action to change oneself or the situation) or *inactive* (e.g., avoiding or denying the source of stress). In general, active strategies are more effective than inactive ones, while both direct and indirect strategies can be constructive (Pines & Aronson, 1988).

The program consisted of five weekly 2-hour workshops that were informal and supportive, and that followed a format of interactive presentation, small/large-group discussion, applications during sessions, and practice between sessions. The content for these sessions targeted three types of coping skills:

1. Skills for Changing the Situation Itself: Situational Coping Skills.

Drawing on management and problem-solving literature, these sessions offered two frameworks for looking at and changing stressful situations by first identifying the changeable aspects and then using a problem-solving approach to develop and carry out an action plan for creating solutions. Participants were also provided specific assertive communication tools for enlisting the cooperation of others in seeking and implementing positive change, and for setting and keeping appropriate limits.

2. Skills for Changing One's Physical Response to the Situation: Physiological Coping Skills.

Stress is fundamentally a form of wear and tear on the body. Thus, we drew on a variety of literature on physiological stress-coping strategies for these sessions. Participants learned both long (30-minute) and very short (30-second) forms of muscle relaxation that can be used for self-renewal in everyday work situations (Woolfolk & Lehrer, 1984). As well, we touched on other physiological approaches for coping with stress (e.g., nutrition and stretching).

3. Skills for Changing How One Thinks About the Situation: Cognitive Coping Skills.

Simply put, much stress happens "between the ears" as a result of our thoughts and beliefs, or cognitions. These sessions drew on cognitive therapy literature and targeted ways to replace self-defeating, self-limiting beliefs with beliefs that are more constructive, realistic, and empowering. Participants learned first to recognize distorted or self-defeating beliefs and then to coach themselves and one another to think differently about themselves or about the situation. Specifically, they coached one another in ways to let go of unrealistic, even tyrannical expectations they held of themselves given the limitations and realities of the situations they faced and to give themselves permission to view their best efforts as good enough. All sessions followed a format of interactive lecture, small-group discussions and role plays, with homework assignments that provided participants the opportunity to try out the skills and new behaviors in their work environments. Each session began with small- and large-group discussion of the experiences gained via the homework assignments, and assignments were turned in for the instructors' review and feedback.

Intervention 2: The Peer Collaboration Program

Because of the apparent value of collegial support in preventing or alleviating job stress and burnout, researchers have advocated creating more regular opportunities for peer support for special education teachers and others in stressful job roles.

Due to its emphasis on supportive, constructive dialogue between professional peers, this intervention seems to have potential for addressing issues of collegial isolation and lack of administrative support among special educators. The Peer Collaboration Program, as originally developed, consisted of training pairs of teachers to use a four-step collegial dialogue to assist each other in identifying and solving student-related problems. For this study, it was modified to apply other work-related problems as well. Via this process, each member of the pair takes a turn as "initiator" (the one presenting a problem) and a "facilitator" (the one providing assistance in problem solving). The four steps were as *follows:*

1. Clarifying. The initiating teacher brings a brief, written description of the problem and responds to clarifying questions asked by the facilitator. This step is the longest of the four [and is] designed to assist the initiating teacher to think of the problem in different or expanded ways. This step continues until the initiating teacher feels that all of the relevant issues have been covered and is ready to move on to summarizing.

2. Summarizing. In this step, the initiating teacher summarizes three facets of the problem being discussed: the specific patterns of behavior that are problematic, the teacher's typical response to them, and the particular aspects of the problem that fall under the teacher's control.

3. Intervention and Prediction. The teachers together generate three possible action plans, and the initiator predicts possible positive and negative outcomes for each one. The initiator then chooses one of the solutions for implementation.

4. Evaluation. The initiator develops a two-part plan to evaluate the solution's effectiveness. The first part consists of a plan to answer the question "Did I do it?" (i.e., implementation of the solution), and the second part consists of ways to answer the question "Did it work?" (i.e., impact on targeted outcomes).

> Participants attended one 3-hour training session in which the process was described, modeled, and practiced with feedback from other participants and from the instructors.

SOURCE: Excerpted from Cooley E., & Yovanoff, P. (1996). Supporting professionals-at-risk: Evaluating interventions to reduce burnout and improve retention of special educators. *Exceptional Children, 62*(4), 336–355.

Reprinted with permission.

SUMMARY

- High levels of prolonged stress lead to teacher dissatisfaction, withdrawal from work, burnout, health problems, and attrition.
- Ideally, efforts should be directed at modifying both the work environment and helping teachers cope with the inevitable stressors they encounter.
- Administrators and teachers should work together to identify major stressors in the environment and work to change those aspects of the environment that are creating stress.
- Stress is influenced by perceptions; thus, helping teachers understand how stress works, the effects of stress, and how they can cope with stress are important.

SELECTED READINGS

Brownell, M. (1997). *Coping with stress in the special education classroom: Can individual teachers more effectively manage stress?* ED414659 ERIC Digest #E545.

Cooley, E., & Yovanoff, P. (1996). Supporting professionals-at-risk: Evaluating interventions to reduce burnout and improve retention of special educators. *Exceptional Children, 62*(4) 336–355.

Howatt, W. A. (2001). *Creating wellness at home and in school.* Bloomington, IN: Phi Delta Kappa Educational Foundation, 1–38.

Luckner, J. L. (1996). Juggling roles and making changes: Suggestions for meeting the challenges of being a special educator. *Teaching Exceptional Children, 28*(2), 22–28.

Wisniewski, L., & Gargiulo, R. M. (1997). Occupational stress and burnout among special educators: A review of the literature. *The Journal of Special Education, 31*(3), 325–346.

WEB SITES

Statewide Center for Healthy Schools

http://www.nyshealthyschools.org/references.htm

This New York Statewide Center supports schools in promoting healthy behaviors and lifestyles for both students and the greater school community.

Stress Burnout: Signs, Symptoms, and Prevention

http://www.helpguide.org/mental/burnout_signs_symptoms.htm

Provides information about preventing stress and burnout.

Strategic Planning for Teacher Quality and Retention

9

To reduce high turnover rates that impose costs on schools, we must improve working conditions, insist on effective teacher preparation, and provide support for new teachers.

(Linda Darling-Hammond, 2003, p. 6)

A leader's framework for teacher retention is presented in Chapter 1 (see Figure 1.1). Reviewing this framework can help school and district leaders consider areas for improvement. Leaders need to assess local conditions and strategically focus on areas that will likely have the greatest impact. School and district leaders need to listen carefully to what teachers say about their work and look for patterns of responses in schools, across the district, and in particular programs.

SCENARIO: LEARNING FROM TEACHERS

In the scenario in Chapter 3, Margaret, the director of special education, wonders why so many special educators are leaving and what principals and administrators can do to hire and keep good teachers. After a discussion with Ennis, Margaret decides to carefully investigate the problem of teacher recruitment and turnover in the district. Margaret and Ennis decide to develop a strategic plan and serve as cochairs in this effort. They know it is important to learn from teachers in the district and to involve them in creating the kinds of environments in which they can do their work well.

CHAPTER OVERVIEW

This chapter discusses ways to better understand what is contributing to attrition and to identify actions that are needed to improve teacher quality and retention. Specifically, this chapter addresses:

- Key questions for understanding school and district attrition, and
- Strategic planning for improving retention.

Several instruments are provided to assess teachers' reasons for leaving and to assess the job satisfaction and commitment of teachers in the district.

KEY QUESTIONS FOR UNDERSTANDING AND IMPROVING RETENTION

Teacher attrition receives much attention in the media and in popular teaching magazines. However, not all districts and schools have problems with teacher attrition. Indeed, some have low attrition rates. Before time and energy is spent "fixing" the attrition problem, it makes sense to develop an understanding of district and school attrition rates, the types of attrition that is occurring, and why it is occurring.

District leaders should begin by "screening" to identify problem areas. The following initial questions are designed to calculate rates of leaving and assess the job satisfaction, commitment, and school climate of the current teaching force.

What Is the District's Special Education Attrition Rate?

The difficulty of calculating an overall attrition rate depends on the databases available in the school system. It is helpful to calculate the rate for more than one year to establish any trends in attrition. In Westover School District, attrition rates increased from 10% of teachers leaving in year one to 15% of teachers in year three. The upward trend is troubling, and if these high rates continue, Westover will have to replace half of its special education teaching force in just a few years.

What Are Patterns in Teacher Attrition and Retention?

Determining the characteristics of those who leave helps direct attention to specific populations. For example what are the characteristics of teachers who leave by race, gender, experience, and position type? How do those who leave compare with those who stay?

For example, in Westover, the average length of district teaching experience for special educators was only seven years—significantly less than the general education average of eighteen years. Understanding this difference helps at least partly explain the higher rates of attrition among beginning special educators, since a particularly young and inexperienced workforce has higher turnover rate than a more experienced workforce. The general educators in Westover left at lower rates than special educators; however, general educators were more likely to *retire* than special educators. Knowing how many teachers will reach retirement age over the next five and ten years is also important information for workforce planning.

Districts and states can use personnel databases to answer some questions. A description of the current workforce and those who have left by race, age, experience, and certification status or types of position (e.g., resource, consulting teaching, exceptionalities taught) can be used to develop a profile of the current district workforce. An understanding of the demographics of the special education teaching force can also help with predicting certain kinds of attrition.

What Are Individual Schools' Attrition Rates?

The personnel databases may be used to summarize teacher characteristics and types of position by school. Attrition rates can also be calculated for each school. In Westover, several schools have particularly high turnover rates.

What Types of Attrition Are Occurring?

Figure 9.1 provides a worksheet to summarize the types of attrition that occur in the district (see Chapter 1 for a discussion of types of attrition). Attrition is divided into those who leave special education teaching but stay in the district and those who leave the district altogether. Although many special education teachers were leaving Westover, Ennis was surprised to learn that about one-third of those who left stayed in the district as general educators.

Figure 9.1 can be modified to address the types of attrition of most interest to the district. Categories can be reduced or added (e.g., how many teachers across specific types of special education programs are leaving).

What Major Factors Contribute to Attrition?

Two major factors contribute to attrition: those unrelated to work and those due to undesirable teaching circumstances. Of course, a combination of factors often contributes to attrition. Exit interviews and surveys are important tools in understanding teachers' reasons for leaving.

Type of Attrition	Definitions of Attrition	Number/ Percentage Leaving in Each Category (Year 1)	Number/ Percentage Leaving in Each Category (Year 2)	Number/ Percentage Leaving in Each Category (Year 3)
District leaver type 1	Retires			
District leaver type 2	Exits teaching altogether			
District leaver type 3	Leaves district, but continues teaching in another system			
District transfer type 1 (stays in special education)	Teachers remain in the same district, but move to different assignment			
District transfer type 2	Transfers to a nonteaching position (e.g., curriculum specialist, administrator)			
District transfer type 3 (leaves special education)	Transfers to a nonspecial education teaching position			
Totals*				

Figure 9.1 District Attrition Analysis Chart

Exit Interviews and Surveys

Exit interviews or surveys should be conducted to assess why special education teachers are leaving the district or transferring to general education positions. The purpose of the exit interview is to obtain information about the special educators' work experience that might otherwise be hard to acquire.

Exit interviews can provide information about how the school district, the school, and the requirements of working in special education are perceived. It is important to ask specific questions concerning how special education teachers perceive their roles, assignments, problems, supports, and successes. Employees who are leaving are likely to be honest about their perceptions of the position (see Resource C for an example of an exit interview).

Ideally, exit interviews will be conducted by the same individual. It is important to select interviewers who listen well and have strong interpersonal skills. The teacher's direct supervisor and principal are not the best individuals to conduct the exit interview. Rather, an individual who is not involved in the central work of the teacher should be selected. In Westover, an individual from the district personnel office was selected to complete exit interviews.

Interviewers need to take time to establish rapport with the teacher. The interviewer should explain the purpose of the interview and let the teacher know how the information will be used. Begin with the easier questions, saving the most difficult questions for the middle or later stage of the interview. Be sure to keep a list of major points.

An alternative to exit interviews is a mailed survey. An interview is usually preferable to a mailed survey because more will be learned and it also gives the opportunity to ask the departing teacher to elaborate on certain responses. If a face-to-face interview is not possible, then mailed surveys can be used to collect information (see Resource D). Before finalizing your interview questions for either an oral or a mailed survey, carefully consider what you hope to learn and ask teachers to review the assessments.

How Do Current Special Educators Feel About Their Work?

An assessment of special educators throughout the district or school provides leaders with a better understanding of how special educators feel about their work, their concerns, what they would like to see changed about their jobs, and their career plans. Such assessments can be used to identify issues that need attention *before* teachers decide to leave. Teachers appreciate the opportunity to share their experiences, especially if they believe the information will be used to improve their work environment.

Teacher Workplace Survey

The Teacher Workplace Survey is a four-page form that can be completed in approximately ten to fifteen minutes (see Resource Section E). This survey includes information on current assignments, items about school climate, teachers' plans to remain, and open-ended items. The open-ended items allow teachers to frame issues that are important to them and to share their own perspectives.

Surveys can be distributed online or mailed to teachers. Current teachers will be unlikely to be candid unless they are guaranteed anonymity; therefore, it is important to state how confidentiality will be handled. Having someone outside the district collect and analyze the surveys usually makes teachers more comfortable in detailing their concerns. Margaret requested that the Workplace Surveys be mailed to a faculty member at the local university.

Teacher background information can be included on the questionnaire or survey. Instruments can be given a code so that the teachers' characteristics can later be merged with the survey responses. The data can be analyzed by school level (e.g., elementary, high school), experience level of the teacher, gender, race, and type of position (e.g., resource, consulting teacher, special class).

STRATEGIC PLANNING FOR RETENTION

Strategic planning can be used to identify areas of need, clarify priorities, and develop action plans to address these needs. In this section, processes and strategies are described for identifying strengths, assessing problems, and formulating action plans to address teacher needs.

Strategic planning requires the use of evaluation tools to learn more about the targeted population and to develop plans to respond to key areas of need. Eight steps are included in strategic planning (modified from Billingsley et al., 1995):

1. Formulate an advisory committee,

2. Develop a mission statement,

3. Develop evaluation purposes and questions,

4. Collect data,

5. Analyze and interpret data,

6. Develop strategic plans,

7. Request resources and form partnerships, and

8. Implement and evaluate the strategic plan.

Strategic planning should consider both short- and long-term goals. It is important to consider a range of factors that influence teacher quality, work conditions, and retention and to consider multiple data sources when making decisions.

Formulate an Advisory Committee

Advisory committees should take responsibility for assessing the current workplace environment and practices, including recruiting and hiring, teacher induction, professional development, investigating promising practices, providing technical assistance, reviewing teachers' work assignments, and assessing needs. These committees can be formed at the school or district levels.

District Level Committee

Margaret and Ennis believe it is important to involve teachers in the district in improving work conditions. They formed an advisory committee to identify issues of importance across the district, develop questions to be answered, consider various data sources, suggest strategies for gathering and analyzing data, help to interpret data findings, and develop strategic plans.

Broad representation from groups with an interest in teacher quality and work conditions is necessary to assure a range of perspectives; at the same time, it is important to keep the committee of a manageable size. At the district level, the advisory committee might involve representatives from any of the following groups:

- Special and general education teachers;
- Principals, associate superintendents;
- Curriculum specialists;
- Parents;
- Community members;
- Paraprofessionals;
- State department personnel; and
- University faculty.

Margaret and Ennis decided on a group of six general and special education teachers, one of each from the elementary, middle, and high schools in Westover City. They included teachers with a range of experience and teachers who worked in different types of settings. They also included an elementary principal, a parent from a local organization, and a university faculty member with expertise in evaluation.

Margaret also realizes the importance of informing the superintendent and local school board of the formation and purposes of the committee. She knows they will be interested in the findings of the group and they are in an important position to provide needed resources.

School Advisory Committees

A school advisory committee may be formed to address general and special educators' needs in the school or an existing school advisory committee may fulfill this purpose. The school committee may identify support needs and raise questions about school policies and practices. The school committee may also want to communicate its needs and concerns to the district advisory committee. Although a school advisory committee will be comprised mainly from members of the specific school, involving a parent and a district office representative can provide additional perspectives and may help secure necessary resources.

Develop a Mission Statement

The advisory committee developed the following mission statement to guide its efforts:

The mission of the Westover Teacher Advisory committee is to ensure the recruitment and retention of a highly qualified teaching force that is ethnically, culturally, and gender balanced. This mission encompasses:

- High performance standards,
- Full and appropriate preparation for teachers,
- Expanded recruitment and systematic hiring processes,
- Continuing development and professional growth throughout the careers of teachers,
- Working conditions and a school climate that focuses on research-based strategies and effective use of instructional time,
- Appropriate supports and necessary resources,
- Incentives that will enhance job satisfaction,
- Involvement of parents, community, and businesses in support of effective teachers and schools (modified from Billingsley et al., 1995).

Develop Evaluation Purposes and Questions

Specific questions need to be answered before a strategic plan can be developed. The committee must assemble any existing reports or data that help it better understand the current status of teacher recruitment and retention in the district. It must also ask what additional information or data are needed. For example:

- What does the district need to learn about teacher recruitment and retention?
- What kinds of data can be gathered to provide information that will answer these questions?

The overall purposes of the evaluation should be stated. The advisory committee should then formulate specific questions to better understand factors that influence teacher quality and contribute to teacher attrition. Figure 9.2 provides examples of questions that might be considered by the committee. The committee will not likely want to address all of these questions; rather, it will want to select those that are most critical in the district. Advisory teams may also want to address other important questions such as diversity issues, follow-up analysis of what teachers do and where they go after leaving, and projected supply and demand issues (e.g., growth in student population).

Westover City Evaluation Purposes and Questions

Margaret, Ennis, and the advisory committee decided that they had little information to draw upon, other than a personnel report indicating that between 10% and 15% of special educators had left over each year for the last three years. They decided to identify several purposes that would help focus their data collection efforts. Their initial list had ten purpose statements, but they narrowed it down to three that they believed were most critical. Below is an example of one purpose statement, a rationale, and their corresponding questions.

Purpose Statement 1: What Is Contributing to Special Education Teacher Attrition in the District?

Rationale: The committee realized that although a recent report from the personnel office indicated it was losing between 10% and 15% of its teachers over the last few years, it did not have any systematic information on why these teachers were leaving. It also was losing approximately one-third of its teachers to general education in Westover; however, it did not have any analyses about why this was occurring. The advisory committee highlighted several questions that it believed would achieve this purpose.

Evaluation Questions for Purpose 1:

a. What percentage of special education teachers are leaving primarily to job dissatisfaction versus other nonwork reasons?

b. What specific work conditions are contributing to dissatisfaction among teachers who leave and the current workforce?

c. What is contributing to transfers from special to general education teaching positions?

d. What patterns are associated with teacher attrition in the district (i.e., experience levels, types of positions, work with particular groups of students)?

| | Examples of Types of Data | | | |
Examples of Evaluation Questions	Personnel Database	Exit Interviews*	Teacher Surveys†	Focus Groups‡
1. What is the overall attrition rate in the district? How do these rates compare to state rates and surrounding district rates?	X			
2. What are the characteristics of the special and general education teaching workforce?	X			
3. What are the characteristics of special and general education teachers who are leaving (e.g., age, gender, race)?	X			
4. Are teachers in any particular types of position more likely to leave (e.g., elementary, secondary; resource, consulting teacher, speech-language pathologist, specific schools)?	X			
5. What reasons do special and general education teachers give for leaving?		X		X
6. To what extent are special educators transferring to general education positions and what are their reasons for these transfers?	X	X		X
7. How many teachers plan to leave the workforce (in one year, three years, and five years)?			X	
8. Based on the current demographics, how many teachers will likely retire over the next five to ten years?	X			

Figure 9.2 Examples of Evaluation Questions and Types of Data

*See Resource C.
†See Resource E.
‡See Resource F.

Figure 9.2 (Continued)

Examples of Evaluation Questions	Examples of Types of Data			
	Personnel Database	Exit Interviews*	Teacher Surveys[†]	Focus Groups[‡]
9. What problems are special educators experiencing in their schools?			X	
10. Do special educators have the knowledge and skills to do their work well?		X	X	X
11. How does the current teacher workforce view various dimensions of their work (e.g., salary/benefits, hiring, induction, professional development, work assignments, perceived stress, overall satisfaction)?			X	
12. What would special educators most like to see changed?		X	X	
13. What concerns do principals have about their leadership of special education teachers and programs?				X

Collect Data

When an evaluation question is stated clearly and specifically, it usually leads to the type of information that will answer it. Margaret, Ennis, and the advisory committee devised a chart to highlight their data collection plan by evaluation question. The four specific types of data that they used are shown in Figure 9.2 and are discussed in more detail below. Westover used personnel databases, the Teacher Workplace Survey, exit interviews, focus groups, and assessments of principals.

Focus Groups

Westover used a focus group to better understand the high rate of transfer from special to general education positions. Rather than interview each of these teachers individually, the advisory committee decided to bring them together for a discussion (see Resource F). Focus groups can provide useful information that is typically more detailed than that collected through surveys.

Focus groups can also be used to follow up on particular problems identified using the Teacher Workplace Survey. For example, collaboration with general education teachers was identified as a problem for special educators in Westover. Two focus groups were then used to learn more about general and special educators' experiences with collaboration. These teachers described the problems they were experiencing in more detail and highlighted ideas for addressing the problems. Several recommendations evolved from the meeting, which included helping principals facilitate collaboration in the schools, providing professional development opportunities to help teachers to learn how to collaborate more effectively, and creating regularly scheduled time for collaboration among general and special education teachers.

Principal Assessments

The advisory committee determined that it needed to better understand principals' perspectives on how special education is working in its schools and principals' needs for professional development. As discussed throughout this book, principals have a critical role to play in enhancing teacher quality and retention in special education. Therefore, learning about their problems and challenges as special education leaders is critical to a well-formulated strategic plan. Learning about the needs of principals can be accomplished through individual interviews, focus groups, or a survey.

Analyze and Interpret Data

Data analyses should be summarized, organized, and displayed in a manner that allows the advisory committee to understand the data. It is beyond the scope of this book to describe the various possible types of data analyses. However, analyses need not be particularly complex or sophisticated to yield valuable information. The readings listed at the end of this chapter include several evaluation books of use in qualitative and quantitative analyses.

Including teacher and teaching position characteristics on surveys can also help with later analysis. For example, if there is high turnover among teachers of students with emotional disorders in the district, an analysis of this particular group (e.g., certification status, work conditions) may be needed. Teacher databases can also be used to identify those who hold special education certification, but are teaching in general education.

Personnel records, exit interviews, teacher workplace surveys, and focus groups provided the advisory committee in Westover with the several data sources that helped to answer a number of their questions. The committee developed an understanding of the nature of attrition, why teachers left, and special educators' perspectives on their work and needed areas of support.

Develop a Strategic Plan

After the data analysis phase was completed, the advisory committee prioritized its concerns. It asked several questions:

How might these concerns be addressed?

Which concerns were best addressed by central office?

Which required school-based efforts?

An example of a strategic plan that resulted from these efforts is presented in Figure 9.3. The plan that resulted from these efforts included goals, corresponding objectives, strategies for meeting the objectives, and the person(s) responsible (see Figure 9.3).

Request Resources and Form Partnerships

Many of the ideas listed in Figure 9.3 represent good administrative practice, such as providing teachers with needed resources and clarifying roles. However, the data and plan also provided the basis for requesting

Goal 1: To ensure an adequate supply of qualified special educators		
Objective(s)	Strategies	Who Is Responsible?
a. Expand recruitment efforts	• Identify five national Web sites for advertising and post descriptions on Web site no later than April 15 • Use job placement services at colleges and universities, especially in surrounding states • Make personal contact with special education programs at universities within a three-hour drive • Increase the number of interns working in special education programs	Director of Special Education
b. Increase opportunities for general educators to work as special educators	• Identify general educators with special education certification and assess interest/provide incentives for moving to special education teaching • Consider online programs and scholarships to fund teachers to switch to special education	Director of Personnel
Goal 2: To improve teacher selection and create good matches between school and teacher		
Objective(s)	Strategies	Who Is Responsible?
a. Decentralize hiring processes	• Develop a revised personnel policy for increasing school involvement in hiring decisions • Provide principal training on screening, interviewing, and selecting qualified special education teachers	Director of Special Education, Director of Personnel, three principals (one from each school level)
b. Evaluate new hiring processes	• Survey newly hired teachers and principals to assess their perceptions on the hiring processes and to solicit recommendations for change • Assess the extent to which new teachers perceive a good job match	Director of Personnel
Goal 3: To improve support of special education teachers		
Objectives	Strategies	Who Is Responsible?
Develop a high-quality teacher mentor program for special educators	• Design a mentoring program using recommendations from Chapter 3 • Secure funding through grants and budget reallocation to train and hire mentors	Director of Special Education, Mentor Coordinating Teacher

Figure 9.3   Strategic Plan for Teacher Recruitment and Retention (Westover City Schools)

Figure 9.3 (Continued)

Objectives	Strategies	Who Is Responsible?
	• Create a "Mentor Coordinating Teacher" position to assist in the development of the mentor program, assist with mentor selection and training, and monitor program's progress during the first year • Provide principals with guidelines for the mentor teaching program and develop a plan for time for new teachers and their mentors to work together	
Increase principal support in special education	• Schedule focus groups to better understand principals' needs in special education leadership and support • Develop a training session for principals including key information and outline special educators' support needs in the district • Encourage principals to discuss special educators' support needs with all special educators in their school • Develop local guidelines for supporting special education teachers • Assess special educators' support needs throughout the district on an annual basis	Principals and Director of Special Education

additional resources. The committee also decided that a closer partnership was needed with universities in the region to help develop induction programs.

Implement and Evaluate the Strategic Plan

The implementation of the plan must be monitored. Assessing the impact of the implemented plan requires that specific questions be addressed. For example:

Is the plan being implemented as designed?

What were the anticipated and unanticipated outcomes from the plan?

What was learned in implementation that will help in future efforts?

SUMMARY

- Leaders can intervene in specific ways to improve teacher retention (see Figure 1 in Chapter 1).
- Assessing local conditions can help focus attention strategically by attending to those aspects that most need change.
- Understanding the particular types of attrition occurring within the district provides information necessary for understanding the inevitable attrition that occurs and improving retention.
- Strategic planning provides insight into teachers' experiences in the district, identifies areas of need, and allows the development of action plans to address these needs.

SELECTED READINGS

Eisner, E. W. (1994). *The educational imagination: On the design and evaluation of school programs* (3rd Ed.). New York: Macmillan.

Krueger, R. A., & Casey, M. A. (2000). *Focus groups: A practical guide for applied research* (3rd Ed.). Thousand Oaks, CA: Sage.

Mertons, D. M., & McLaughlin, J. (2003). *Research and evaluation methods in special education.* Thousand Oaks, CA: Corwin Press.

Sanders, J. R. (1994). *The program evaluation standards: How to assess evaluations of educational programs.* The Joint Committee on Standards for Educational Evaluation. Thousand Oaks, CA: Sage.

WEB SITES

American Evaluation Association (AEA)

http://www.eval.org/
The AEA is designed to improve and support evaluation practices and methods.

Institute of Educational Sciences (IES)

http://www.ed.gov
The IES is designed to advance the field of education research by encouraging the use of evidence-based education. The institute consists of the National Center for Education Research, the National Center for Education Statistics, and the National Center for Education Evaluation and Regional Assistance.

Part IV

Resources

Resource A: Principal Support Questionnaire

Please indicate the extent to which your principal supports you by circling one number for each item.

	No Extent	A Small Extent	Some Extent	Great Extent
1. Acts friendly toward me	1	2	3	4
2. Is easy to approach	1	2	3	4
3. Gives me undivided attention when I am talking	1	2	3	4
4. Is honest and straightforward with the staff	1	2	3	4
5. Gives me a sense of importance and that I make a difference	1	2	3	4
6. Considers my ideas	1	2	3	4
7. Allows me input into decisions that affect me	1	2	3	4
8. Supports my decisions	1	2	3	4
9. Shows genuine concern for my program and students	1	2	3	4
10. Notices what I do	1	2	3	4
11. Shows appreciation for my work	1	2	3	4
12. Treats me as one of the faculty	1	2	3	4

	No Extent	A Small Extent	Some Extent	Great Extent
13. Gives clear guidelines regarding job responsibilities	1	2	3	4
14. Provides standards for performance	1	2	3	4
15. Offers constructive feedback after observing my teaching	1	2	3	4
16. Provides frequent feedback about my performance	1	2	3	4
17. Helps me evaluate my needs	1	2	3	4
18. Trusts my judgment in making classroom decisions	1	2	3	4
19. Shows confidence in my actions	1	2	3	4
20. Provides helpful information for reducing stress	1	2	3	4
21. Provides information on research-based practices	1	2	3	4
22. Provides knowledge of current legal policies	1	2	3	4
23. Provides opportunities for me to grow professionally	1	2	3	4
24. Encourages professional growth	1	2	3	4
25. Provides suggestions for me to improve instruction	1	2	3	4
26. Identifies resource personnel to contact for specific problems he or she is unable to solve	1	2	3	4
27. Assists in identifying special education students	1	2	3	4
28. Is available to help when needed	1	2	3	4
29. Helps me establish my schedule	1	2	3	4
30. Helps me solve problems and conflicts that occur	1	2	3	4

	No Extent	A Small Extent	Some Extent	Great Extent
31. Facilitates communications between general and special educators	1	2	3	4
32. Helps me with student discipline problems	1	2	3	4
33. Helps me with parent issues	1	2	3	4
34. Provides time to complete my nonteaching responsibilities (e.g., IEPs, conferences)	1	2	3	4
35. Provides adequate planning time	1	2	3	4
36. Provides teaching materials, space, and resources	1	2	3	4
37. Participates in child study/eligibility/IEP meetings/parent conferences	1	2	3	4
38. Works with me to plan specific goals and objectives for my program and students	1	2	3	4
39. Provides extra assistance when I become overloaded	1	2	3	4
40. Equally distributes resources and unpopular chores	1	2	3	4

SOURCE: Adapted from the Special Education Teacher Support questionnaire in Littrell, P., Billingsley, B., & Cross, L. (1994). The effects of principal support on special and general educators' stress, job satisfaction, school commitment, health, and intent to stay in teaching, *Remedial and Special Education*, 15(5), 297-310.

Resource B: Teacher Concerns Inventory

Michael J. Fimian

Note: A text version of this inventory and manual are available for use without charge from The Teacher Stress Inventory Web site: http://www.instructionaltech.net/tsi/

This instrument should be administered only after a thorough study of the material on the Web site, including the manual, which includes important information about administering, scoring, and interpreting the results of this inventory.

The following is a list of teacher concerns. Please identify the factors that cause you stress in your present position. Read each statement carefully and decide if you ever feel this way about your job. Then, indicate how strong the feeling is when you experience it by circling the appropriate rating on the five-point scale. If you have not experienced this feeling, or if the item is inappropriate for your position, circle number "1" (no strength; not noticeable). The rating scale is shown at the top of each page.

Examples:

I feel insufficiently prepared for my job.	1	2	3	4	5

If you feel very strongly that you are insufficiently prepared for your job, circle number "5."

I feel that if I step back in either effort or commitment, I may be seen as less competent.	1	2	3	4	5

If you never feel this way, and the feeling does not have noticeable strength, circle number "1."

HOW STRONG?	1	2	3	4	5
	no strength, not noticeable	mild strength, barely noticeable	medium strength, moderately noticeable	great strength, very noticeable	major strength, extremely noticeable

TIME MANAGEMENT					
1. I easily overcommit myself.	1	2	3	4	5
2. I become impatient if others do things too slowly.	1	2	3	4	5
3. I have to try doing more than one thing at a time.	1	2	3	4	5
4. I have little time to relax/enjoy the time of day.	1	2	3	4	5
5. I think about unrelated matters during conversations.	1	2	3	4	5
6. I feel uncomfortable wasting time.	1	2	3	4	5
7. There isn't enough time to get things done.	1	2	3	4	5
8. I rush in my speech.	1	2	3	4	5
Add items 1 through 8; divide by 8; place your score here:					
WORK-RELATED STRESSORS					
9. There is little time to prepare for my lessons/responsibilities.	1	2	3	4	5
10. There is too much work to do.	1	2	3	4	5
11. The pace of the school day is too fast.	1	2	3	4	5
12. My caseload/class is too big.	1	2	3	4	5
13. My personal priorities are being short changed due to time demands.	1	2	3	4	5
14. There is too much administrative paperwork in my job.	1	2	3	4	5
Add items 9 through 14; divide by 6; place your score here:					
PROFESSIONAL DISTRESS					
15. I lack promotion and/or advancement opportunities.	1	2	3	4	5
16. I am not progressing in my job as rapidly as I would like.	1	2	3	4	5
17. I need more status and respect on my job.	1	2	3	4	5
18. I receive an inadequate salary for the work I do.	1	2	3	4	5

	1	2	3	4	5
19. I lack recognition for the extra work and/or good teaching I do.	1	2	3	4	5
Add items 15 through 19; divide by 5; place your score here:					

DISCIPLINE AND MOTIVATION

I feel frustrated . . .

20. . . . because of discipline problems in my classroom.	1	2	3	4	5
21. . . . having to monitor pupil behavior.	1	2	3	4	5
22. . . . because some students would be better if they tried.	1	2	3	4	5
23. . . . attempting to teach students who are poorly motivated.	1	2	3	4	5
24. . . . because of inadequate/poorly defined discipline problems.	1	2	3	4	5
25. . . . when my authority is rejected by pupils/administration.	1	2	3	4	5
Add items 20 through 25; divide by 6; place your score here:					

PROFESSIONAL INVESTMENT

26. My personal opinions are not sufficiently aired.	1	2	3	4	5
27. I lack control over decisions made about classroom/school matters.	1	2	3	4	5
28. I am not emotionally/intellectually stimulated on the job.	1	2	3	4	5
29. I lack opportunities for professional improvement.	1	2	3	4	5
Add items 26 through 29; divide by 4; place your score here:					

EMOTIONAL MANIFESTATIONS

I respond to stress . . .

30. . . . by feeling insecure.	1	2	3	4	5
31. . . . by feeling vulnerable.	1	2	3	4	5
32. . . . by feeling unable to cope.	1	2	3	4	5
33. . . . by feeling depressed.	1	2	3	4	5
34. . . . by feeling anxious.	1	2	3	4	5
Add items 30 through 34; divide by 5; place your score here:					

FATIGUE MANIFESTATIONS

I respond to stress . . .

35. . . . by sleeping more than usual.	1	2	3	4	5

36. . . . by procrastinating.	1	2	3	4	5
37. . . . by becoming fatigued in a very short time.	1	2	3	4	5
38. . . . with physical exhaustion.	1	2	3	4	5
39. . . . with physical weakness.	1	2	3	4	5

Add items 35 through 39; divide by 5;
place your score here:

CARDIOVASCULAR MANIFESTATIONS

I respond to stress . . .

40. . . . with feelings of increased blood pressure.	1	2	3	4	5
41. . . . with feeling of heart pounding or racing.	1	2	3	4	5
42. . . . with rapid and/or shallow breath.	1	2	3	4	5

Add items 40 through 42; divide by 3;
place your score here:

GASTRONOMICAL MANIFESTATIONS

I respond to stress . . .

43. . . . with stomach pain of extended duration.	1	2	3	4	5
44. . . . with stomach cramps.	1	2	3	4	5
45. . . . with stomach acid.	1	2	3	4	5

Add items 43 through 45;
divide by 3; place your score here:

BEHAVIORAL MANIFESTATIONS

I respond to stress . . .

46. . . . by using over-the-counter drugs.	1	2	3	4	5
47. . . . by using prescription drugs.	1	2	3	4	5
48. . . . by using alcohol.	1	2	3	4	5
49. . . . by calling in sick.	1	2	3	4	5

Add items 46 through 49;
divide by 4; place your score here:

TOTAL SCORE

Add all calculated scores; enter the value here _____

Then, divide by 10; enter the Total Score here _____

Demographic Variables

Your gender:

Number of years you have taught: _____

Your age: _____

How many students do you teach each day? _____

What level students do you teach? (circle the rest of your answers)

    Elementary   Middle School   Secondary

Which is the most advanced degree you have?

    Bachelor's   Master's   Doctorate

Which type of position do you hold?

    Special Educator   General Educator

Do you and your peers support one another when needed?	Yes	No
Do you and your supervisors support one another when needed?	Yes	No

SOURCE: Teacher Stress Inventory, by Michael J. Fimian. Used with permission.

Resource C: Teacher Exit Interview

Purpose:

To understand reasons for special education attrition in the school or district.

To understand how the school, the district, and the requirements of working in special education are perceived.

Conducting the interview:

- Take time to establish rapport.
- Save difficult questions for the end.
- Ask the teacher if he or she would mind if you take notes.
- Stay focused on the teacher and record major points.
- Minimize your own comments.

Questions:

1. How did you feel about working in this school district? In your school?

2. What did you like most about teaching in special education?

3. What did you like least?

4. What would you recommend to improve the work conditions in this position?

5. How did you view the compensation that you received in this district?

6. How did you feel about each of these aspects of your job?
   a. Experiences during the hiring and interview process
   b. Support and mentoring during your first year(s)

    c. School-based support and assistance that you receive

    d. District-based support and assistance

    e. Your professional development opportunities

    f. Your job responsibilities

    g. Your satisfaction and overall well-being on the job

7. Are there any conditions under which you would have stayed? If yes, what would those conditions be?

8. What led to your decision to leave your position?

9. Overall, on a scale from 1 (lowest) to 10 (highest), how would you rate your satisfaction with your special education teaching position?

10. Would you recommend this district (school) to others?

11. Do you have another position? If yes: How does the new job compare with the one in your current school?

12. Is there anything else you would like to share?

Resource D: Teacher Follow-up Questionnaire

Last Year's Teaching Assignment

1. Area(s) of student exceptionalities taught last year:

   _____

2. School level(s) taught last year (circle one or more):
   _____ Pre-K
   _____ Elementary
   _____ Middle
   _____ High School
   _____ Other

3. Circle the type of position that you held last year (circle only one):
   a. Consulting teacher
   b. Resource
   c. Combined resource/self-contained
   d. Self-contained
   e. Other (Specify): _____

Reasons for Leaving

4. Which of the following is the major reason that you left your teaching position? (circle one main reason)
   a. Personal reason(s) unrelated to work
   b. To retire
   c. To pursue another education-related career
   d. To pursue a career outside of education

    e. For better salary or benefits

    f. For a better teaching assignment

    g. Dissatisfaction with job

    h. Other (Specify): _____

If you had a "second" or "third" important reason for leaving, select each additional reason from the above listing and record the corresponding letter (a–h)

_____ Second Important Reason _____ Third Important Reason

5. Did you indicate reason "g" (dissatisfaction with job in question 4 above as *one* of your reasons for leaving? (circle one).

    a. Yes (Proceed to question 6)

    b. No (Skip to question 8)

6. Listed below are several areas of dissatisfaction that might contribute to a teacher's decision to leave special education teaching. What were your *major* reasons for leaving your position last year?

    (Circle only those that were important to your decision to leave your position.)

a. Poor opportunity for professional advancement

b. Inadequate support from central administration

c. Inadequate support from principal(s)

d. Lack of adequate support staff (e.g., aides, clerical assistants)

e. Inadequate facilities or classrooms

f. Unsafe working environment

g. Lack of influence over school/district policies and practices

h. Lack of control over own classroom

i. Inappropriate placement of students with disabilities

j. Inadequate program design or curriculum

k. Lack of student progress

l. Lack of sense of accomplishment

m. Demands of working with special education students

n. Class size/caseload too large

o. Student discipline problems

p. Poor relations and interactions with other teachers

q. Too much paperwork

r. Too many nonteaching responsibilities

s. Monotony/routine of job

t. Poor salary and fringe benefits

u. Lack of challenge/opportunities for growth

v. Lack of appreciation/respect

w. Problems with parents

x. Stress associated with teaching

y. Other (Specify): _____

7. From the areas of dissatisfaction presented in question 6 above, select the one that was most important to your decision to leave teaching and record the corresponding letter (a–y) below.

   _____ Most important area of dissatisfaction

If you want to comment on any of the areas in which you were dissatisfied, please do so below.

Incentives to Stay

8. Is there any action that the school system could have taken to convince you to remain in your position?

   (Circle One)

   a. Yes (Proceed to question 9)
   b. No   (Skip to question 10)

9. List below, as specifically as possible, the actions that would have convinced you to stay in your former position.

Teacher Preparation and Experience

10. What is the *highest* degree you have earned?

    (Circle One)

    a. BA or BS
    b. Master's
    c. EdS
    d. PhD or EdD

11. Which of the following best describes your preparation for teaching?

    a. fully certified for position
    b. not certified for position

12. How many total years have you taught (omitting any partial years of teaching)?

    _____ Years

Thank you for completing this questionnaire. Please return in the enclosed envelope.

Adapted from: Billingsley, B., Pyecha, J., Smith-Davis, J., Murray, K., & Hendricks, M. (1995). *Improving the Retention of Special Education Teachers: Final Report.* (Prepared for Office of Special Education Programs, Office of Special Education and Rehabilitative Services, U.S. Department of Education, under Cooperative Agreement H023Q10001). (ERIC Document Reproduction Service No. ED379860).

Resource E: Teacher Workforce Survey

Part A: Climate Survey

Please circle the response choice that best reflects your experience.

	Not at All	Small Extent	Moderate Extent	Great Extent
The school administration's behavior toward the staff is supportive and encouraging.	1	2	3	4
Necessary materials are available when you need them.	1	2	3	4
Routine duties and paperwork are reasonable and do not interfere with my teaching.	1	2	3	4
Your principal enforces school rules for student conduct and backs you when you need it.	1	2	3	4
Most of your colleagues share your beliefs and values about what the central mission of the school should be.	1	2	3	4
The principal knows the type of school he or she wants and has communicated this vision to the staff.	1	2	3	4
There is a great deal of cooperative effort among the staff members.	1	2	3	4
Staff members in this school are recognized for jobs well done.	1	2	3	4
You make a conscious effort to coordinate the content of your courses with that of other teachers.	1	2	3	4

	Not at All	Small Extent	Moderate Extent	Great Extent
Teachers participate in making most of the important educational decisions in this school.	1	2	3	4
The special education division supports you in your interactions with parents.	1	2	3	4
Your principal backs you up when needed.	1	2	3	4
You can count on your principal or vice principal to provide appropriate assistance when a student or child's behavior requires it.	1	2	3	4
The special education division backs you up when needed.	1	2	3	4
You really like the school in which you are currently working.	1	2	3	4
You feel included in what goes on in this school.	1	2	3	4
Your job provides you with opportunities to learn new things.	1	2	3	4

Part B: Reasons for Wanting to Stay in or Leave Your Current Special Education Teaching Position

Your responses to the next two items will help us understand your desire to either stay in or leave your current special education teaching position. Please respond to item 1 if you want to stay in your current position, and respond to item 2 if you want to leave your current position.

1 If you want to *stay in* your current teaching position, please list your most important reasons.

2. If you want to *leave* your current special education teaching position, please list your most important reasons.

Part C: Plans to Remain

Please check the one answer that most closely indicates your plans at this point in time.

How long do you plan to remain in special education teaching in this district?

____ Plan to leave as soon as possible.

____ Plan to leave in the next year or two.

_____ Plan to stay 5 years.
_____ Plan to stay 10 years.
_____ Plan to stay longer than 15 years.
_____ Plan to stay until retirement.

Part D: Background Information

1. School Level
_____ Elementary _____ Middle _____ High School

2. Years of Teaching Experience _____

3. Type of Position
_____ Consulting _____ Resource _____ Combined _____ Special
Class/School

Thank you for your help! Please return in the enclosed postage-paid envelope.

SOURCE: Items 1–16 of the climate survey were developed for use in the Study of Personnel Needs in Special Education (SPeNSE). The original instrument and study reports can be viewed online at: http://ferdig.coe.ufl.edu/spense/SPeNSECLEANService Provider_FinalCATI.doc

Part B adapted from Billingsley et al., 1995.

Resource F: Conducting Focus Group Interviews

Focus groups can be used for many different purposes. The open-ended questions for this particular interview were designed to help school and district administrators better understand the high rate of transfer from special to general education. Other focus groups might address the induction of special educators, the support needs of special educators, collaboration issues, or administrative support.

1. Create a comfortable environment and provide time to establish rapport. Provide refreshments and allow time at the beginning of the meeting for participants to talk informally.

2. Clarify the purpose(s) of the focus interview. For example, "All of the teachers in this group were special educators, but moved to general education teaching. We are interested in know more about your transfer to general education."

3. Discuss procedures for the interview. The session leader should: discuss the use of notes and recordings (if used), and explain how the information will be used; provide assurances and constraints regarding confidentiality; and answer questions.

4. Redirect the group to the questions if the conversation becomes sidetracked.

5. Use open-ended probes to encourage contribution from all group members, such as, "Are there other things that are important?" "Are there other perspectives?" or "Does anyone else in the group have other ideas?" When only general ideas are stated, the leader may ask, "Would you elaborate on that?" or "Please share an example."

6. End the interview with an opportunity for each member to share a final idea or make a summary statement.

7. Thank all participants for their participation.

Examples of Interview Questions:

1. Why did you initially become a special educator?

2. What were your most important reasons for transferring to general education positions?

3. Were there any other reasons for leaving your special education position?

4. How has teaching in general education teaching differed for you from special education teaching?

5. Would there have been any incentives that might have kept you in special education teaching?

6. Would you consider transferring back to special education teaching? Why or why not?

7. Do you have any recommendations for strategies the district might use to retain special education teachers?

Note: For more information, see: Krueger, R. A., & Casey, M. A. (2000). *Focus Groups: A Practical Guide for Applied Research* (3rd Ed.). Thousand Oaks, CA: Sage.

References

A Distinction That Matters: What School Board Members Should Know About National Board Certification. (2004). Retrieved February 20, 2004 from http://www.nbpts.org/pdf/distincschoolboard.pdf

A High-Quality Teacher for Every Classroom (SPeNSE Factsheet). (2002). Retrieved January 20, 2004 from http://ferdig.coe.ufl.edu/spense/Summary Report serviceproviders.pdf

American Association for Employment in Education (AAEE). (2000). *Educator supply and demand.* Columbus, OH: Author.

Addressing the revolving door: How to retain your special education teachers (Star Legacy Module). (2002). Retrieved March 22, 2004 from http://iris.peabody.vanderbilt.edu/retention/chalcycle.htm

Arends, R., & Rigazio-DiGilio, A. J. (July 2000). *Beginning teacher induction: Research and examples of contemporary practice.* Paper presented at the Annual Meeting of the Japan-United States Teacher Education Consortium, Tokyo, Japan.

Bateman, D., & Bateman, F. (2001). *A principal's guide to special education.* Arlington, VA: Council for Exceptional Children.

Benner, A. D. (2000). *The cost of teacher turnover.* Austin, TX: Texas Center for Educational Research.

Billingsley, B. (2004). Special education teacher retention and attrition: A critical analysis of the research literature. *The Journal of Special Education, 38*(1), 39-55.

Billingsley, B., Carlson, E., & Klein, S. (2004). The working conditions and induction support of early career special educators. *Exceptional Children, 70*(3), 333-347.

Billingsley, B., & Cross, L. (1991). Teachers' decisions to transfer from special to general education. *The Journal of Special Education, 24*, 496-511.

Billingsley, B., Pyecha, J., Smith-Davis, J., Murray, K., & Hendricks, M. (1995). *Improving the retention of special education teachers: Final report.* (Prepared for Office of Special Education Programs, Office of Special Education and Rehabilitative Services, U. S. Department of Education, under Cooperative Agreement H023Q10001). (ERIC Document Reproduction Service No. ED379860).

Billingsley, B. S. (1993). Teacher retention and attrition in special and general education: A critical review of the literature. *The Journal of Special Education, 27*(2), 137-174.

Billingsley, B. S. (2002). *Beginning special educators: Characteristics, qualifications, and experiences.* Retrieved March 11, 2004 from http://ferdig.coe.ufl.edu/spense/IHEsummaryfinal.doc

Billingsley, B. S., Bodkins, D., & Hendricks, M. B. (1993). Why special educators leave teaching: Implications for administrators. *Case in Point, 7*(2), 23-38.

Billingsley, B. S., & Cross, L. H. (1991). Teachers' decisions to transfer from special to general education. *The Journal of Special Education, 24*(4), 496-511.

Billingsley, B. S., & Cross, L. H. (1992). Predictors of commitment, job satisfaction, and intent to stay in teaching: A comparison of general and special educators. *The Journal of Special Education, 25*(4), 453-471.

Billingsley, B. S., & Tomchin, E. M. (1992). Four beginning LD teachers: What their experiences suggest for trainers and employers. *Learning Disabilities Research and Practice, 7,* 104-112.

Boe, E. E., Barkanic, G., & Leow, C. S. (1999). *Retention and attrition of teachers at the school level: National trends and predictors.* Philadelphia, PA: University of Pennsylvania, Graduate School of Education, Center for Research and Evaluation in Social Policy.

Boe, E., Bobbitt, A. S., Cook, L., & Barkanic, G. (1998). *National trends in teacher supply and turnover* (Data analysis report no. 1998 DAR1). Philadelphia, PA: University of Pennsylvania, Graduate School of Education, Center for Research and Evaluation in Social Policy.

Boe, E. E., Bobbitt, A. S., Cook, L. H., Whitener, S. D., & Weber, A. L. (1997). Why didst thou go? Predictors of retention, transfer, and attrition of special and general education teachers from a national perspective. *The Journal of Special Education, 30*(4), 390-411.

Bondy, E., & Brownell, M. T. (2004). Getting beyond the research to practice gap: Researching against the grain. *Teacher Education and Special Education, 27*(1), 47-56.

Boyer, L., & Gillespie, P. (2000). Keeping the committed: The importance of induction and support programs for new special educators. *Teaching Exceptional Children, 33*(1), 10-15.

Boyer, L., & Lee, C. (2001). Converting challenge to success: Supporting a new teacher of students with autism. *The Journal of Special Education, 35*(2), 75-83.

Brewster, C., & Railsback, J. (2001). *Supporting beginning teachers: How administrators, teachers, and policymakers can help new teachers succeed.* Portland, OR: Northwest Regional Educational Laboratory.

Brownell, M. (1997). *Coping with stress in the special education classroom: Can individual teachers more effectively manage stress?* Retrieved April 15, 2004 from http://www.ericfacility.net/ericdigests/ed414659.html

Brownell, M., Hirsch, E., & Seo, S. (2004). Meeting the demand for highly qualified special education teachers during severe shortages: What should policymakers consider? *The Journal of Special Education, 38*(1), 22-38.

Brownell, M. T., Smith, S. W., McNellis, J., & Miller, M. D. E. (1997). Attrition in special education: Why teachers leave the classroom and where they go. *Exceptionality, 7*(3), 143-155.

Brownell, M. T., Yeager, E., Rennells, M. S., & Riley, T. (1997). Teachers working together: What teacher educators and researchers should know. *Teacher Education and Special Education, 20*(4), 340-359.

Burrello, L. C., Lashley, C., & Beatty, E. E. (2001). *Educating all students together: How school leaders create unified systems.* Thousand Oaks, CA: Corwin.

Carlson, E., & Billingsley, B. (2001, July). *Working conditions in special education: Current research and implications for the field.* Paper presented at the OSEP Project Directors' Conference, Washington, DC.

Carlson, E., Brauen, M., Klein, S., Schroll, K., & Willig, S. (2002). *Key findings from the study of personnel needs in special education.* Bethesda, MD: WESTAT.

Cohen, M. K., Gale, M., & Meyer, J. M. (1994). *Survival guide for the first-year special education teacher* (Revised Ed.). Arlington, VA: Council for Exceptional Children.

Cooley, E., & Yovanoff, P. (1996). Supporting professionals-at-risk: Evaluating interventions to reduce burnout and improve retention of special educators. *Exceptional Children, 62*(4), 336-355.

Covey, S. R. (1989). *The 7 habits of highly effective people.* New York: Simon & Schuster.

Crockett, J. B. (1999-2000). Viable alternatives for students with disabilities: Exploring the origins and interpretations of the least restrictive environment. *Exceptionality, 8*(1), 43-60.

Crockett, J. B. (2002). Special education's role in preparing responsive leaders for inclusive schools. *Remedial and Special Education, 23*(3), 157-168.

Crockett, J. B. (2004). Taking stock of science in the schoolhouse: Four ideas to foster effective instruction. *The Journal of Learning Disabilities, 37*(3), 189-199.

Cross, L. H., & Billingsley, B. (1994). Testing a model of special educators' intent to stay in teaching. *Exceptional Children, 60*(5), 411-421.

Darling-Hammond, L. (2003). Keeping good teachers: Why it matters, what leaders can do. *Educational Leadership, 60*(8), 6-13.

Darling-Hammond, L., & Youngs, P. (2002). Defining "highly qualified teacher": What does "scientifically-based research" actually tell us? *Educational Researcher, 31*(9), 13-35.

Davies, J., Davies, R., & Heacock, S. (2003). A wellness program for faculty. *Educational Leadership, 60*(8), 68-70.

DiPaola, M. F., & Walther-Thomas, C. (2003). *Principals and special education: The critical role of school leaders* (No. COPSSE Document No. IB-7). Gainesville, FL: University of Florida, Center on Personnel Studies in Special Education.

Diversifying the special education workforce: Special education workforce watch. (2004). Center for Personnel Studies in Special Education (No. PB-10), Gainesville, FL: University of Florida.

Dooley, E. A. (2003). Increasing the number of ethnically diverse faculty in special education programs: Issues and initiatives. *Teacher Education and Special Education, 26*(4), 264-272.

Educational Testing Services. (2004). http://www.ets.org/praxis/

Eisner, E. W. (1994). *Educational imagination: On the design and evaluation of school programs* (3rd Ed.). New York: Macmillan.

Embich, J. L. (2001). The relationship of secondary special education teachers' roles and factors that lead to professional burnout. *Teacher Education and Special Education, 24*(1), 58-69.

Enlarging the pool: How higher education partnerships are recruiting and supporting future special educators from underrepresented groups. (2003). Retrieved October 10, 2003 from http://www.special-ed-careers.org/pdf/enlargingthepool.pdf

The ERIC/OSEP Special Project (2002). *To light a beacon: What administrators can do to make schools successful for all students.* Retrieved May 22, 2004 from http://www.ericec.org/osep-sp.html

Farber, B. A. (2000). Treatment strategies for different types of teacher burnout. *Psychotherapy in Practice, 56*(5), 675-689.

Feiman-Nemser, S., Schwille, S., Carter, C., & Yusko, B. (1999). *A conceptual review of literature on new teacher induction.* Washington, DC: National Partnership for Excellence and Accountability in Teaching.

Fimian, M. J. (1988). *Teacher Concerns Inventory.* Retrieved April 24, 2004 from http://www.instructionaltech.net/tsi/

Frampton, P., Vaughn, V. L., & Didelot, J. M. (2003). The professional development school partnership: Is practice improving? Teachers and principals respond. *The Journal of Educational Administration, 41*(3), 292-309.

Frank, A. R., & McKenzie, R. (1993). The development of burnout among special educators. *Teacher Education and Special Education, 16*(2), 161-170.

Friend, M., & Cook, L. (2003). *Interactions: Collaboration skills for school professionals* (4th Ed.). Boston: Allyn & Bacon.

Fuchs, D., & Fuchs, L. S. (1998). Researchers and teachers working together to adapt instruction for diverse learners. *Learning Disabilities Research and Practice, 13*(3), 126-137.

Fuchs, L. S. (2003). Assessing treatment responsiveness: Conceptual and technical issues. *Learning Disabilities Research and Practice, 18,* 172-186.

Geiger, W. L., Crutchfield, M. D., & Mainzer, R. (2003). *The status of licensure of special education teachers in the 21st century.* Retrieved October 20, 2003 from http://www.coe.ufl.edu/copsse/pubfiles/RS-7.pdf

General education teachers' role in special education (SPeNSE Factsheet). (2001). Retrieved March 2, 2004 from http://ferdig.coe.ufl.edu/spense/gened11-29.pdf

George, N. L., George, M. P., Gersten, R. & Grosenick, J. R. (1995). To leave or to stay? An exploratory study of teachers of students with emotional and behavioral disorders. *Remedial and Special Education, 16*(4), 227-236.

Gersten, R., & Dimino, J. (2001). The realities of translating research into classroom practice. *Learning Disabilities Research & Practice, 16,* 120-130.

Gersten, R., Gillman, J., Morvant, M., & Billingsley, B. (1995). *Teachers' Perceptions of Working Conditions: Problems Related to Central Office Support.* Paper presented at the National Dissemination Forum on Issues, Special Education Teacher Satisfaction, Retention, and Attrition (ERIC Document Reproduction Service No. ED 389 155).

Gersten, R., Keating, T., Yovanoff, P., & Harniss, M. K. (2001). Working in special education: Factors that enhance special educators' intent to stay. *Exceptional Children, 67*(4), 549-567.

Gersten, R., Vaughn, S., Deshler, D., & Schiller, E. (1997). What we know about using research findings: Implications for improving special education practice. *Journal of Learning Disabilities, 30*(5), 466-476.

Gibb, G., & Welch, M. (1998). The Utah mentor teacher academy: Evaluation of a statewide mentor program. *Teacher Education and Special Education, 21*(1), 22-33.

Gold, Y. (1996). Beginning teacher support: Attrition, mentoring, and induction. In J. Sikula, T. J. Buttery, & E. Guyton (Eds.), *Handbook of Research on Teacher Education* (2nd Ed., pp. 548-594). New York: Simon & Schuster.

Goor, M. B., Schwenn, J. O., & Boyer, L. (1997). Preparing principals for leadership in special education. *Intervention in the School and Clinic, 32*(3), 133-141.

Greer, J. G., & Greer, B. B. (1992). Stopping burnout before it starts: Prevention measures at the preservice level. *Teacher Education and Special Education, 15*(3), 168-174.

Griffin, C. C., Winn, J. A., Otis-Wilborn, A., & Kilgore, K. L. (2002). *New teacher induction in special education.* Gainesville, FL: University of Florida, Center on Personnel Studies in Special Education.

Guskey, T. R. (2003). Analyzing lists of the characteristics of effective professional development to promote visionary leadership. *NASSP Bulletin, 87,* 4-20.

Guzman, N. (1997). Leadership for successful inclusive schools: A study of principal behaviours. *Journal of Educational Administration, 35*(5), 439-450.

Hawley, W., & Valli, L. (1999). The essentials of effective professional development: A new consensus. In L. Darling-Hammond & G. Sykes (Eds.), *Teaching as a Learning Profession: Handbook of Policy and Practice* (pp. 127-152). San Francisco, CA: Jossey-Bass Publishers.

Hertzog, H. S. (2002). "When, how, and who do I ask for help?" Novices' perceptions of problems and assistance. *Teacher Education Quarterly, 29*(3), 25-41.

Hope, W. C. (1999). Principals' orientation and induction activities as factors in teacher retention. *Clearinghouse, 73*(1), 54-56.

Howatt, W. A. (2001). *Creating Wellness at Home and in School.* Bloomington, IN: Phi Delta Kappa Educational Foundation.

Hughes, R. E. (2001). Deciding to leave but staying: Teacher burnout, precursors and turnover. *International Journal of Human Resource Management, 12*(2), 288-298.

Idol, L. (1997). Key questions to building collaborative and inclusive schools. *The Journal of Learning Disabilities, 30*(4), 384-394.

Implementing IDEA: A Guide for Principals. (2001). Arlington, VA: Council for Exceptional Children and the National Association of Elementary School Principals, ILIAD Project.

Individuals with Disabilities Education Act Amendments. (1997). 20 U.S.C., 1400, et seq.

Ingersoll, R. M. (2001). Teacher turnover and teacher shortages: An organizational analysis. *American Educational Research Journal, 38*(3), 499-534.

Ingersoll, R. M., & Smith, T. M. (2003). The wrong solution to the teacher shortage. *Educational Leadership, 60*(8), 30-33.

Johnson, S. M., & Birkeland, S. E. (2003a). Pursuing a sense of success: New teachers explain their career decisions. *American Educational Research Journal, 40*(3), 581-617.

Johnson, S. M., & Birkeland, S. E. (2003b). The schools that teachers choose. *Educational Leadership, 60*(8), 20-24.

Johnson, S. M., & Kardos, S. M. (2002). Keeping new teachers in mind. *Educational Leadership, 59*(6), 12-16.

Kaff, M. S. (2004). Multitasking is multitaxing: Why special educators are leaving the field. *Preventing School Failure, 48*(2), 10-17.

Kilgore, K. L., Griffin, C., Otis-Wilborn, A., & Winn, J. (2003). The problems of beginning special education teachers: Exploring the contextual factors influencing their work. *Action in Teacher Education, 25*(1), 38-47.

Klingner, J. K. (2004). The science of professional development. *The Journal of Learning Disabilities, 37*(3), 248-255.

Klingner, J. K., Ahwee, S., Pilonieta, P., & Menendez, R. (2003). Barriers and facilitators in scaling up research-based practices. *Exceptional Children, 69*(4), 411-429.

Klingner, J. K., & Vaughn, S. (2002). The changing roles and responsibilities of an LD specialist. *Learning Disability Quarterly, 25*, 19-31.

Kozleski, E., Mainzer, R., & Deshler, D. (2000). *Bright Futures for Exceptional Learners: An Action Agenda to Achieve Quality Conditions for Teaching and Learning.* Reston, VA: Council for Exceptional Children.

Krueger, R. A., & Casey, M. A. (2000). *Focus Groups: A Practical Guide for Applied Research* (3rd Ed.). Thousand Oaks, CA: Sage.

Lambert, L. (1998). *Building Leadership Capacity in Schools.* Alexandria, VA: Association for Supervision and Curriculum Development.

Lambert, L. (2002). Beyond instructional leadership: A framework for shared leadership. *Educational Leadership, 59*(8), 37-40.

Lashley, C., & Boscardin, M. L. (2003). *Special education administration at a crossroads: Availability, licensure, and preparation of special education administrators.* (COPSSE Document No. IB-8). (Gainesville, FL: University of Florida, Center on Personnel Studies in Special Education.

LeCompte, D., & Dworkin, A. G. (1991). *Giving up on school: Student dropouts and teacher burnouts.* Newbury Park, CA: Corwin Press.

Levin, J., & Quinn, M. (2003). *Missed opportunities: How we keep high-quality teachers out of urban classrooms.* Retrieved October 14, 2003 from http://www.tntp.org/report.html

Little, M. E., & Houston, D. (2003). Research into practice through professional development. *Remedial and Special Education, 24*(2), 75-87.

Littrell, P., Billingsley, B., & Cross, L. (1994). The effects of principal support on special and general educators' stress, job satisfaction, school commitment, health, and intent to stay in teaching, *Remedial and Special Education, 15*(5), 297-310.

Liu, E. (April 2003). *New teachers' experiences of hiring: Preliminary findings from a four-state study.* Paper presented at the American Educational Research Association, Chicago, Illinois.

Local administrator's role in promoting teacher quality (SPeNSE Factsheet). (2002). Retrieved January 5, 2004 from http://ferdig.coe.ufl.edu/spense/administrator summary.pdf

Luckner, J. L. (1996). Juggling roles and making changes: Suggestions for meeting the challenges of being a special educator. *Teaching Exceptional Children, 28*(2), 22-28.

MacDonald, V. (2001). Making time: A teacher's report on her first year of teaching children with emotional disabilities. *The Journal of Special Education, 35*(2), 84-91.

Mainzer, R., & Horvath, M. (2001). *Issues in preparing and licensing special educators.* Reston, VA: Council for Exceptional Children.

Mandlawitz, M. (2003). *A Tale of 3 cities: Urban perspectives on special education.* Washington, DC: Center on Education Policy.

Mariage, T. V., & Garmon, M. A. (2003). A case of educational change: Improving student achievement through a school-university partnership. *Remedial and Special Education, 24*(4), 215-234.

Maroney, S. A. (2000). What's good? Suggested resources for beginning special education teachers. *Teaching Exceptional Children, 33*(1), 22-27.

Maslach, C., Jackson, S., & Leiter, M. P. (1996). *Maslach Burnout Inventory* (3rd Ed.). Palo Alto, CA: Consulting Psychologists Press.

Mastropieri, M. A. (2001). Is the glass half full or half empty? Challenges encountered by first-year special education teachers. *The Journal of Special Education, 35*, 66-74.

McLaughlin, M., & Nolet, V. (2004). *What every principal needs to know about special education.* Thousand Oaks, CA: Corwin.

McLeskey, J., Tyler, N., & Flippin, S. S. (2004). The supply of and demand for special education teachers: A review of research regarding the nature of the chronic shortage of special education teachers. *The Journal of Special Education, 38*(1), 5-22.

McLeskey, J., & Waldron, N. L. (2002). Professional development and inclusive schools: Reflections on effective practice. *The Teacher Educator, 37*(3), 159-173.

Mertons, D. M., & McLaughlin, J. (2003). *Research and evaluation methods in special education.* Thousand Oaks, CA: Corwin.

Myers, S. (2004). *An illustration of the work lives of experienced teachers of students with emotional and/or behavioral disorders at the middle school level.* Unpublished dissertation, Virginia Tech, Blacksburg, VA.

Miller, M. D., Brownell, M., & Smith, S. W. (1999). Factors that predict teachers staying in, leaving, or transferring from the special education classroom. *Exceptional Children, 65*(2), 201-218.

Moir, E., & Bloom, G. (2003). Fostering leadership through mentoring. *Educational Leadership, 60*(8), 58-60.

Morvant, M., Gersten, R., Gillman, J., Keating, T., & Blake, G. (1995). *Attrition/retention of urban special education teachers: Multi-faceted research and strategic action planning. Final Performance Report, Volume 1* (No. ERIC Document Reproduction Service No. ED338154). Eugene, OR.

National boards set standards for teachers and the field. (2004, April-June). *CEC Today, 10*(1), 5, 17.

National Staff Development Council's Revised Standards for Staff Development. (2001). Retrieved January 5, 2004 from http://www.nsdc.org/standards/collaborationskills.cfm

NCATE. (2004). *What is a professional development school?* Retrieved February 20, 2004 from http://www.ncate.org/pds/standards/what_is.htm

New No Child Left Behind flexibility: Highly qualified teachers (Factsheet). Retrieved June 1, 2004 from http://www.ed.gov/nclb/methods/teachers/hqtflexibility.pdf

No Child Left Behind Act of 2001. (H.R.1), Title II (2002).

No Child Left Behind: Toolkit for teachers. (2003). Retrieved October 3, 2003 from http://www.ed.gov/teachers/nclbguide/nclb-teachers-toolkit.pdf

Oregon Special Education Recruitment and Retention Project: Support for new teachers. (2004). Retrieved January 6, 2004 from http://www.tr.ccou.edu/rrp/teacher support.htm.

Paperwork in special education (SPeNSE Factsheet). (2002). Retrieved December 19, 2003 from http://ferdig.coe.ufl.edu/spense/Paperwork.doc

Pritchard, F., & Ancess, J. (1999). *The effects of professional development schools: A literature review.* Retrieved February 13, 2004 from http://www.ericsp.org/pages/digests/EffectsofProfDev.htm

Recruiting and retaining high-quality teachers (SPeNSE Factsheet). (2002). Retrieved February 5, 2004 from http://ferdig.coe.ufl.edu/spense/policymaker5.pdf

Rice, E. H. (2002). The collaboration process in professional development schools: Results of a meta-ethnology, 1990-1998. *Journal of Teacher Education, 53*(1), 55-67.

Rice, E. H., & Afman, H. (2002). The facilitators of and barriers to the collaboration process in professional development schools. In I. N. Guadarrama, J. Ramsey, & J. L. Nath (Eds.), *Forging Alliances in Community and Thought.* Greenwich, CT: Information Age Publishing.

Rosenberg, M. S., Griffin, C. C., Kilgore, K. L., & Carpenter, S. L. (1997). Beginning teachers in special education: A model for providing individualized support. *Teacher Education and Special Education, 20*(4), 301-321.

Rosenberg, M. S., O'Shea, L., & O'Shea, D. (1998). *Student teacher to master teacher.* New York: Macmillan.

Rosenberg, M. S., & Sindelar, P. T. (2001). *The proliferation of alternative routes to certification in special education: A critical review of the literature.* Arlington, VA: The National Clearinghouse for the Professions in Special Education.

Rowley, J. B. (1999). The good mentor. *Educational Leadership, 56*(8), 20–22.

Sanders, J. R. (1994). *The program evaluation standards: How to assess evaluations of educational programs.* The Joint Committee on Standards for Educational Evaluation. Thousand Oaks, CA: Sage.

Schnorr, J. M. (1995). Teacher retention: A CSPD analysis and planning model. *Teacher Education and Special Education, 18*(1), 22-38.

Silent crisis. Retrieved June 1, 2004 from http://www.rnt.org/channels/clearing house/becometeacher/121_teachershort.htm

Singer, J. D. (1992). Are special educators' career paths special? Results from a 13-year longitudinal study. *Exceptional Children, 59*(3), 262-279.

Singh, K., & Billingsley, B. (1996). Intent to stay in teaching: Teachers of students with emotional disorders versus other special educators. *Remedial and Special Education, 17*(1), 37-47.

South Carolina Teacher Cadet Program. Retrieved February 9, 2004 from www.cerra.org/teachercadet-directory.asp

Special education teaching conditions must be improved. (2000, June/July). *CEC Today, 6*, 1.

Stronge, J. H., & Hindman, J. L. (2003). Hiring the best teachers. *Educational Leadership, 60*(8), 48-52.

Supporting beginning special educators (Star Legacy Module). (2004). Retrieved March 22, 2004 from http://iris.peabody.vanderbilt.edu/beginteach/chal cycle.htm

Trautman, M. L. (2004). Preparing and managing paraprofessionals. *Intervention in the School and Clinic, 39*(3), 131-138.

Tyler, N., Yzquierdo, Z., Lopez-Reyna, N., & Flippin, S. S. (2004). Cultural and linguistic diversity and the special education workforce: A critical overview. *The Journal of Special Education, 38*(1), 22-38.

United States Department of Education. (2001). *Twenty-third annual report to Congress on the implementation of the Individuals with Disabilities Education Act.* Washington, DC: Author.

Vaughn, S., Hughes, M. T., Schumm, J. S., & Klingner, J. (1998). A collaborative effort to enhance reading and writing instruction in inclusion classrooms. *Learning Disability Quarterly, 21*, 57-74.

Voltz, D. L. (2001). Preparing general education teachers for inclusive settings: The role of special education teachers in the professional development school context. *Learning Disability Quarterly, 24*, 288-296.

Walther-Thomas, C., Korinek, L., McLaughlin, V. L., & Williams, B. (2000). *Collaboration for inclusive education: developing successful programs.* Boston: Allyn & Bacon.

Weiss, M. P., & Lloyd, J. W. (2002). Congruence between roles and actions of secondary special educators in co-taught and special education settings. *The Journal of Special Education, 35*, 58-68.

Westling, D. L., & Cooper-Duffy, K. (2003). The Western Carolina University Teacher Support Program: A multi-component program to improve and retain special educators. *Teacher Education and Special Education, 26*(2), 154-158.

Westling, D. L., & Whitten, T. M. (1996). Rural special education teachers' plans to continue or leave their teaching positions. *Exceptional Children, 62*, 319-335.

Whitaker, S. D. (2000a). Mentoring beginning special education teachers and the relationship to attrition. *Exceptional Children, 66*(4), 546-566.

Whitaker, S. D. (2000b). What do first-year special education teachers need? Implications for induction programs. *Teaching Exceptional Children, 33*(6), 28-36.

Whitaker, S. D. (2003). Needs of beginning special education teachers: Implications for teacher education. *Teacher Education and Special Education, 26*(2), 106-117.

White, M., & Mason, C. (2001). *Mentoring induction principles and guidelines.* Retrieved October 2, 2002 from http://www.cec.sped.org/spotlight/udl/mip_g_manual_11pt.pdf

Williams, J. S. (2003). Why great teachers stay. *Educational Leadership, 60*(8), 71-77.

Wisniewski, L., & Gargiulo, R. M. (1997). Occupational stress and burnout among special educators: A review of the literature. *The Journal of Special Education, 31*(3), 325-346.

Youngs, P. (January 2003). *State and district policy related to mentoring and new teacher induction in Connecticut:* Stanford University. Prepared for the National Commission on Teaching and America's Future.

Zabel, R. H., & Zabel, K. (2001). Revisiting burnout among special education teachers: Do age, experience, and preparation still matter? *Teacher Education and Special Education, 24*, 128-139.

Feedback About *Cultivating and Keeping Committed Special Educators*

I am interested in your feedback about this book and how it could be improved. Please send your comments to Bonnie S. Billingsley via e-mail to bbilling@vt.edu or via post to 309 War Memorial Hall, Virginia Tech, Department of Teaching and Learning, Blacksburg, VA 24061-0313.

Your position: _____

Strengths of book:

Suggested improvements:

Other comments:

Index

Note: Page numbers in *italics* indicate figures or boxed text.

A Joint Publication

CEC: Leading the Way

The Council for Exceptional Children, a private nonprofit membership organization, was established in 1922. CEC is an active network of more than 55,000 members in the United States, Canada, and over 30 countries and is the largest professional organization internationally committed to improving educational outcomes for individuals with exceptionalities. CEC accomplishes its worldwide mission on behalf of educators and others working with children with exceptionalities by advocating for appropriate government policies; setting professional standards; providing continuing professional development; and assisting professionals to obtain conditions and resources necessary for effective professional practice.

**CORWIN
PRESS**

The Corwin Press logo—a raven striding across an open book—represents the union of courage and learning. Corwin Press is committed to improving education for all learners by publishing books and other professional development resources for those serving the field of K–12 education. By providing practical, hands-on materials, Corwin Press continues to carry out the promise of its motto: **"Helping Educators Do Their Work Better."**